Innocence Lost

In an ultimate sense, certainly, something is predecided for all human practice, namely that the individual as well as society is oriented towards "happiness". That appears a natural, manifestly reasonable statement. But we must concede to Kant that happiness, this ideal of the imagination, cannot be satisfactorily defined. Practical reason demands, however, that we think about our ends with just as much precision as about their corresponding means; that is, in our actions we can consciously prefer one way of acting over another and ultimately subordinate one purpose to another. Far from simply presupposing a given order of social life and making our practical choices within that given framework, in every decision we make we are responsive to a consistency of quite a different kind.

Hans-Georg Gadamer, *Truth and Method*, 1960

Innocence Lost

Islamism and the Battle over Values and World Order

Lars Erslev Andersen

Translated by
Lea Pedersen & Rune Reimer Christensen

University Press of Southern Denmark
2007

© The author and University Press of Southern Denmark 2007
Author's website: www.erslev-andersen.dk
Set by DTP-Funktionen, University of Southern Denmark

Printed by Narayana Press

ISBN 97-887-7674-200-3

The translation of this book was made possible by a grant from
the University of Southern Denmark.

Cover illustration:
US helicopter on a mission in the Middle East. Scanpix.

University of Southern Denmark Studies in History and Social Sciences vol. 340

University Press of Southern Denmark
Campusvej 55
DK-5230 Odense M
Phone: +45 6615 7999
Fax: +45 6615 8126
Press@forlag.sdu.dk
www.universitypress.dk

Distribution in the United States and Canada:
International Specialized Book Services
5804 NE Hassalo Street
Portland, OR 97213-3644 USA
www.isbs.com

Distribution in the United Kingdom:
Gazelle
White Cross Mills
Hightown
Lancaster
LA1 4XS
U.K.
www.gazellebooks.co.uk

Contents

Preface 7

The Battle over Values, the Muhammad Cartoon Case,
and the Unfinished Rushdie Affair 11
– The Islamist Battle over Values 15
– Madonna, Schiffer and Rushdie 24

Part 1: Regime Change as Strategy
– Democracy as Shock Therapy in the Middle East 38
– Iraq – A Collapsed State 61
– Hamas, Hariri and Iran 75

Part 2: The Democratic Dilemma in the Authoritarian Middle East
– Limits to Freedom? 94
– The Democratic Deficit in the Middle East: Four Theories 97
– Middle Eastern Globalization Strategies 105
– Are All People Equal? 121

Part 3: The Globalization of Al-Qaida's Battle over Values
– Al-Qaida: From Organization to Ideology 126
– Jihad on the Internet: Local Networks 143
– Terrorism in Denmark? 151

Towards a Global Civil War? 157
– Theory of the Partisan 160
– Limits to World Order 163

Postscript 169
– After Lebanon: A New Cold War in the Middle East 169

Bibliography 179

Notes 187

Preface

The controversy surrounding *Jyllands-Posten*'s drawings of the Prophet Muhammad changed the international image of Denmark and consequently the way in which Danes perceive themselves. Denmark lost its innocence. The burning of Danish flags, assaults on Danish embassies, and the boycotting of Danish goods indicate that Danish identity underwent a considerable change in the early months of 2006. There are at least three sides to this story: First, how it went from being solely a Danish matter to being an important issue internationally. This development involves the Danish government's handling of the matter, the role played by Danish imams in the dissemination of the issue throughout the Middle East, the role played by Middle Eastern governments, and the Friday sermons and statements given throughout January 2006 by the head of the al-Azhar Mosque in Cairo and the Grand Mufti of Mecca. Other circumstances may have influenced the situation, but certainly a number of questions remain to be answered. Opposition groups in *Folketinget* (the Danish parliamentary assembly) have promised us an independent inquiry into these matters. Whether or not such an inquiry actually comes about, the matter will undoubtedly become the subject of future historical research. Secondly, why twelve drawings published in a Danish newspaper could lead to fatal violence and mass demonstrations, and their consequences, in the Islamic world. The issue here is politics rather than offended religious sensibilities, a battle over values. This battle is being fought in the Islamic world as well as in the conflict between Islamism and Western democratic order which plays a significant role in the war on terror. This war unfortunately seems to create more and greater problems than it solves. This book offers a possible explanation of why this matter developed so dramatically in terms of political consequences, through a discussion of the preconditions for the war on terror, for the project of the democratization of the Middle East, and for the opposition this project faces in the region. At issue is the clash between an idealistic vision of a new world order and the necessities of *realpolitik* which arise with its implementation, and the consequences of that clash in terms of the legitimacy of our Middle East policy. Thirdly, a question arises concerning the possible long-term consequences of the controversy in terms of Denmark's position in international relations in general and particularly in the Middle East. So far these questions remain the subject of conjecture, but answers begin to take shape when the issue of why the Muhammad cartoon controversy had such an inflammatory effect in the Middle East is examined. This book constitutes one such examination.

According to the German philosopher Hegel, the Owl of Minerva takes flight at dusk, by which he meant that it is easier to know of that which has come to pass than of that which will come to pass. This is obviously true, and I will not pretend to have had any idea that the incident of the *Jyllands-Posten* drawings would develop in such a dramatic manner. I did not! I had not imagined that it would land Denmark in its worst foreign policy crisis since the Second World War. I find it unlikely that anyone else expected this, although some will undoubtedly claim to have foreseen these dramatic developments; in a similar manner, an increasing number of people proudly claim to have foreseen the fall of the Berlin Wall, although significantly their predictions were voiced only after the Wall had come down. After the fact, it makes sense to discuss why it was possible for things to develop the way they did. We must turn our attention to the Middle East, to the war on terror, and to Iraq.

This book discusses the struggle for order in the Middle East, which takes place at the intersection of idealistic vision and the necessities of *realpolitik*. These clash because the necessities of *realpolitik* usually undermine idealism's requirements of legitimacy. In the introductory chapter the battle over values is described, the concept of community of interpretation is introduced, and three cases which predate that of the Muhammad drawings are discussed. Of these three cases the unfinished Rushdie affair is certainly the more serious. The main body of the text is divided into three parts. The first part gives an account of the change in U.S. national security policy after September 11, including the George W. Bush administration's vision of a new

Middle East policy as well as an in-depth analysis of the war in Iraq; the background, course, and aftermath of the war, and the significance of the war in relation to developments in Iraq and in the Middle East, focusing on Palestine, Syria and Iran. The second part consists of a discussion of the philosophical and theoretical basis for the war on terror, involving four different theories on the lack of democracy in the Middle East which are contrasted with four different Middle Eastern strategies for adjusting to the post-September 11 world. In part three I leave the subject of the revolutionary attempts on the part of the US at democratizing the Middle East through the war on terror, and consider the militant opposition to this strategy and the changes which terrorism and Islamism have undergone since the bombings of the Al-Qaida headquarters in the Tora Bora mountains in Afghanistan in 2001. In my concluding remarks I pose the question of whether the world is headed towards a global civil war reminiscent of the protracted wars that ravaged Europe in the 16th and 17th centuries. The overall theme is the confrontation between Islamism and Western order, how it manifests itself in the Middle East, and its significance for the Western order itself. The subject of the book is not the *Jyllands-Posten* drawings of Muhammad, rather it seeks to explain the background of the controversy it created in the Middle East. In other words, this book discusses why some drawings in a Danish newspaper could lead to Denmark's loss of innocence on the international stage.

I would like to thank the Managing Director of the University Press of Southern Denmark, Thomas Kaarsted, for supporting this project from its inception in February, that is, writing a book about the context of the Muhammad cartoon case. I would also like to thank Assistant Professor Gunna Funder Hansen, Center for Middle Eastern Studies, University of Southern Denmark, for her able assistance with the Danish edition, and Ph.D. candidate Philipp C. Bleek, Georgetown University, Washington, D.C. for proofreading the translation. A warm thanks to my translators Lea Pedersen and Rune Reimer Christensen for their diligent work and kind cooperation. I would furthermore like to thank my graduate students at the Center for Middle Eastern Studies and undergraduate students in the Department of History at the University of Southern Denmark for listening to and participating in discussions of my views. My most loving thoughts go to Ingeborg and Frederik for helping me find the time to write this book in the busy schedule of our everyday life. While I am aware that parts of this book are polemical, it is well-intentioned. I wish to contribute to the discussion concerning the role of Denmark in Middle East politics now that our innocence has been lost. The book was written during the Cartoon affair in February and March 2006.

London, February 2007

The Battle over Values, the Muhammad Cartoon Case, and the Unfinished Rushdie Affair

Express yourself
(You've got to make him)
Express himself
Hey, hey, hey, hey
So if you want it right now, make him show you how
Express what he's got, oh baby ready or not
Express yourself
(You've got to make him)
So you can respect yourself
Hey, hey
So if you want it right now, then make him show you how
Express what he's got, oh baby ready or not

Madonna & Stephen Bray

A distinction can be made between an incident and an event. An incident is an occurrence which does not essentially change our perception of ourselves in the world. Our understanding of the world and of ourselves is left unchanged by the incident. Denmark's decision to participate in the war in Iraq was an incident. Although obviously it became a subject of debate, was harshly criticized by some and enthusiastically supported by others, our self-image remained basically unchanged. The Ministry of Foreign Affairs made changes to its travel warnings in response to incidents which had taken place in countries such as Egypt and Palestine, for instance a terrorist attack in the holiday resort area of Sharm al-Shaikh or an escalation of the conflict between Palestinians and Israelis. Once the situation had settled down, we would again be able to travel to these areas expecting to be received with the same sympathetic understanding with which people in the Middle East have customarily received Danes: they have considered us innocent and peaceful, and in their minds we have been associated mainly with Lurpak butter. While we were indeed at war in Iraq, this was taking place far removed from Danish society, and that endeavor was primarily a project of the Danish government. Whether we supported or opposed the war, it changed so little in terms of our self-image that it never even became an issue in the February 2005 general election, which was mostly focused on the question of how to spend our wealth.

The publication of the drawings of the Prophet Muhammad in *Jyllands-Posten* in September 2005 likewise constituted an incident. It was subject to debate, protests were made by governments, international organizations, Muslims in Denmark, and Islamists in the Middle East. The general impression, however, seemed to be that this too would pass, and that we could safely persist in our understanding of ourselves as innocent and well-liked by all – in spite of our participation in the war on terror. We expected the matter to have been defused once Prime Minister Anders Fogh Rasmussen in his New Year's speech had expressed respect for religions other than our own, and Minister for Foreign Affairs Per Stig Møller had conferred with the Arab League and the Organization of the Islamic Conference (OIC), which is comprised of fifty-six Islamic countries.

Two weeks later the incident became an event.

Imams of Middle Eastern mosques, particularly in Saudi Arabia, encouraged a boycott on Danish goods. The head of the influential al-Azhar Mosque in Cairo, Sheikh Sayed Mohammed Tantawi, the Grand Mufti of Saudi Arabia, Sheikh Abdul Aziz al-Shaikh, and Qatar University professor, the Egyptian sheikh Yusuf al-Qaradawi, who hosts his own television show on the *al-Jazeera* satellite network, all called for punitive measures against *Jyllands-Posten*. This message sounded throughout the Arab countries, spreading throughout the Islamic world, forcing Arab governments to respond. Saudi Arabia recalled its ambassador from Copenhagen, Libya closed its People's Bureau in the Danish capital, Jordanian parliamentarians passed resolutions calling for a response from the King of Jordan, and a trade boycott spread. Still, the expectation remained that the unrest would come to an end, that Danish butter would probably soon return to Arab supermarket shelves, and that we would once more be able to travel to the Middle East and find ourselves being associated mainly with Arla dairy products.

But when the Danish Embassy in Damascus was set aflame – or, rather, the house in which the embassy inhabits the third floor – and the Danish Embassy Office in Beirut came under a similar attack the following day, the case of the Muhammad drawings had become an event. From that point on, the very nature of our image as Danes had changed. The burning of Danish flags, and of likenesses of Anders Fogh Rasmussen, changed the way we are perceived. Our image as nice, friendly and peaceful people was replaced by an understanding of us which is in keeping with what we actually are, and have been for quite some time: A nation at war, allied to the United States and Israel. The understanding of the Danish nation had, as poignantly described by a Danish professor of political science, moved from the logic of peace to the logic of war.[1] Denmark has lost its innocence, and the way in which all things Danish are perceived in the Middle East has undergone a radical change. This event forces us to change the way we perceive ourselves, and the way in which we understand our own place and part in the world. When the case of the Muhammad drawings became an event, Danish identity itself changed. It has become a part of the battle over values which is taking place in the Middle East and between the West and the Islamic world. Our identity, then, is not solely determined by the battle over values which is taking place in Denmark, which for instance finds expression in peculiar phenomena such as an officially approved, prescriptive cultural canon. It is also influenced by the battle over values which is taking place within the Middle Eastern order, a struggle which is, among other things, concerned with determining the role of Islam within this order. As a participant in the coalition of the willing in the war on terror, we are actively assuming a part in this Middle Eastern battle over values, and this bears upon our struggle over a Danish national order. This has long been the case, but it took twelve drawings in a Danish newspaper to make us aware of it. Danish identity as such, then, is not merely a Danish concern, but it is also affected by the battle over values that is being fought in the Middle East. Even if all Muslim immigration to Denmark was brought to a halt, and all Muslims now living here were deported, that would in no sense change the fact that the fight for the Muslim soul unavoidably plays a part in the present struggle over Danish identity and Danish values.

This book examines the effects which the global battle over values has on the Middle East, and the ramifications of Western efforts to fight terror by military as well as peaceful means, which involve us as active agents in the struggle to determine which values will bring on a new, or at least different, Middle Eastern order. The concept of 'order' signifies a cohesion which is organized on the basis of a shared set of values, which are borne out on three different levels: Firstly, in terms of the way in which life is actually lived and organized socially; secondly, in terms of the statutes of the community; and, thirdly, in terms of the idealistic vision of the good life on which the values of the community are based. What characterizes an order is, on the one hand, a shared set of basic values, and, on the other, a delimitation of the order in question, separating it from others. An example would be the Western order, based on a particular understanding of freedom, rights and democracy, differentiating it from other orders which do not organize themselves in accordance with these basic values. On all three levels a struggle is taking place over the right or true interpretation of the basic values, and changes on any one level will affect the other levels. This means that the concrete realization of idealistic visions will result in changes with regards to both the statutes of the order in question, such as its constitution, and to the way in which life is actually conducted. The construal of the basic values of a particular order is dynamically related to the construals of other orders: the struggle to determine the right or true construal of the concept of freedom of expression is intensified when, as in connection with the case of the Muhammad drawings, it is challenged by the construal put forth by another order, one which considers freedom of expression to be subordinate to religious values. The interpretative struggle to determine upon which values a given order should be based is conducted on all levels, from the everyday struggles of ordinary life through the dense sphere of political life and into the realm of international relations. Under certain circumstances this struggle emerges in the form of acts of violence, as in cases when a state punishes criminals for the purpose of maintaining order, or when groups or organizations resort to terrorism with the intention of fighting the prevailing order. The risk that a battle over values will develop into a violent situation is reduced proportionately to the strength and extent of a consensus concerning the shared basic values within an order. The risk of violence, terrorism, civil war and inter-regional wars grows if agreement concerning the understanding of shared values is weakened. The interpretation or understanding of values, and the struggle to bring these to bear within a given order, is thus not merely an intellectual concern, but is a part of social, cultural and political everyday life and of the battles that take place here.

The Islamist Battle over Values

We are currently witnessing a battle over values within Muslim communities throughout the world, communities within which criticism of Western liberal values is widespread and pronounced. In the 2005 elections in Egypt, Islamic fundamentalists affiliated with the Muslim Brotherhood seized the opportunity to strengthen their representation in parliament, which resulted in the reform process being brought to a halt. Jordan is hesitant to reform its electoral act due to the fear that such reforms would lead to a strengthening of Islamist forces in future elections. In Syria, an increasingly weakened regime justifies its continued desperate retention of power with the argument that the prevailing regime constitutes the sole alternative to fundamentalist Islamic forces. It is likely the Islamists who command the greater popular appeal among the populations of all three countries. In Saudi Arabia, already a fundamentalist state, the most vehemently conservative Islamists won the greater number of seats in the strictly monitored 2005 local elections; and in Kuwait, the position of the Islamist opposition, which is critical of the process of reform that, for instance, in 2005 introduced women's suffrage, is stronger than ever before.

An escalating battle over values is likewise taking place elsewhere. In Yemen a plethora of Islamist institutions and organizations are emerging, which increasingly transform mosques into political battlegrounds for Islamist propaganda, and in Iran a conservative Islamic apocalypticist who openly speaks for the destruction of Israel and denies the Holocaust was elected president by the Iranian voters. In Palestine, the Islamist Hamas movement won the 2006 election and assumed the leadership of the Palestinian Authority. In Iraq, a well-orchestrated Sunni Muslim rebellion resists the attempts of the Western coalition to introduce democracy, and a Shia Muslim majority insists upon their interpretation of Islamic law, *sharia*, as the basis for an Iraqi state which they are determined will not be a secular one. Many members of Muslim immigrant communities in Europe, including Denmark, actively participate in the battle over values which is being fought in the Middle East and South Asia, concerning the potential political role of Islam in the establishment of a Middle Eastern order.

In all these places, forces for reform are at work. Elections have been held in each country, albeit in some places they have had the appearance of travesties of free and democratic elections. Throughout these areas, opposition to reforms is on the rise. The underlying reasons differ and relate to local circumstances. There is no basis for postulating a unified, Islamist fundamentalist opposition. Even in Gaza, in Iraq, in Yemen, in Syria and in Egypt, Islamism is fragmented and divided into various fundamentalist construals of the true Islamic state. There is, however, general agreement throughout these areas on certain matters: about condemning as hypocritical the policies of the West and the United States towards Palestine; about taking a skeptical stance towards the intentions of the West in connection with its efforts to spread democracy, in their opinion a strategy which makes possible the exploitation and oppression of Muslim peoples and countries; and that true, basic political values are to be found through a political interpretation of Islam. For the Islamists the war on terror primarily constitutes an attempt on the part of the West at achieving dominance by waging war on Muslims and their faith.

Several different circumstances are regarded as confirmation of these convictions: The West applauds the Israeli withdrawal from the West Bank, but meanwhile Israel is constructing a wall which fences in the Palestinians and systematically subverts any possibility of the realization of a Palestinian state; Muslims are locked up at Guantanamo without any semblance of due process; Iraqis are being tortured as part of the process of establishing a state of Iraq governed by law; in the name of democracy, Yemen is supported while its government carries out a massacre on the Yemenite population in the Northern part of the country; Saudi Arabia is commended for being tough on terrorists without making any efforts to supplement the numerous killings with rights and liberties for the people; Western countries are implementing legislation against terrorism which is perceived as aimed primarily at Muslims; on the basis of their names and beliefs, Muslims are to a large extent shut out of labor markets in the West; Muslims are being transported by secret CIA aircraft, to be interrogated and detained in secret prisons; our right to freedom of expression is absolute and inviolable where criticism of Islam is concerned, but less so pertaining to Islamist criticism of democracy, and so forth. Well-intentioned individuals and politicians in the West have offered explanations along the following lines: anti-terrorism legislation is not aimed at Muslims as such, the West, led by the USA, still supports the notion of a Palestinian state, and the torture that has taken place at Abu Ghraib was the work of a few bad apples within the U.S. Army. But these explanations leave Islamists unmoved. In their view, Western liberal values entail a justification for oppressing and waging war on Islam. This does not constitute a marginal attitude, limited to a small, extremist group of fanatics. It is an understanding which is widespread and deeply rooted in Middle Eastern populations.

The Drawings of the Prophet

Jyllands-Posten's drawings of the Prophet Muhammad serve as a Maggi cube in relation to the Islamist battle over values: It contains everything, and when dissolved under the right conditions it makes it possible for all kinds of criticisms, ranging from questions concerning criticism of religion under the auspices of freedom of expression to the clash of civilizations, to unfold. Anyone can make use of this Maggi cube for their own political purposes, and what is even worse is that it always points in the opposite direction, away from the critic himself and towards 'the other' or others: For *Jyllands-Posten* it points to the imams and the cultural leftists, for Danish Islamists it points to right wing groups and the government, for the cultural leftists it points to *Dansk Folkeparti* (Danish People's Party) and the harsh tenor of the immigration debate, for Islamists in Arab countries it points to the West's demands for political reform, and for the Iraqi resistance movement it points to the presence of coalition forces in their country. And for beleaguered dictatorial Arab regimes, this Maggi cube is welcomed as a means of making Denmark the symbolic center of attention in an effort to divert Islamist criticism away from themselves and, instead, towards the West. This is exactly what happened when the struggling Syrian government allowed the Islamists to express their rage, by not preventing their attack on the Danish embassy. Such diversional tactics have been used before. In the 1970's, the Saudi Arabian government was facing mounting internal Islamist criticism, criticism which culminated when in 1979 a group of Islamists occupied the Grand Mosque in Mecca. At that point, the United States' support for and funding of the Islamist resistance to Soviet occupation forces in Afghanistan was a godsend. They were now able to send their critics to Afghanistan while at the same time supporting the holy war against the Russian infidels. This lasted until the Soviet Union gave in and the Saudi Islamists returned to the kingdom; here, however, support for their opposition remained in force, and they were now able to gain backing for al-Qaida's battle against the American infidels.

Jyllands-Posten's drawings of the Prophet have become a means for such diversions. A grossly politicized campaign on the part of radical Danish imams, beleaguered Arab regimes needing to divert Islamist criticism away from themselves, and a hesitant and confused political reaction on the part of the Danish government and the Danish population – who could never have imagined the extreme political potency of this Maggi cube – combined to "unleash uncontrollable forces," in the words of Anders Fogh Rasmussen. Whether or not the Danish government made mistakes in its handling of the Muhammad case, it is worth considering whether it was purely coincidental that it just happened to be a Danish matter which turned out to be a useful diversion, or whether its being Danish made it so? One might suspect that the fact that Denmark is such a small country may have made it a convenient target for the unleashing of these uncontrollable forces. The cost of a potential backlash against the Middle Eastern countries would presumably be negligible compared to those resulting from a conflict with a larger country. This view seems to be borne out by the reluctant responses on the part of the European Union and the United States, and, as will become clear, two of the countries which play significant parts in the affair, Egypt and Saudi Arabia, received almost no noteworthy international criticism, which for the most part was aimed at Iran and Syria. In the light of the intense battle over values in the Middle East, one might also consider whether the conflict was in fact triggered by the offence against religious sensibilities attributable to *Jyllands-Posten's* drawings, or whether they just happened to offer an opportunity for a politically engineered diversion, in a situation where a conflict involving the unleashing of uncontrollable forces was due regardless? Whatever the case may be, the frustration and anger which was expressed in connection with the Muhammad controversy ensues from the battle over values taking place in the Middle East and South Asia, a battle which has long been a characteristic of the political situation in the region.

The Islamist battle over values has many proponents outside of the Middle East, in parts of Africa, in Indonesia, in the Philippines, in Chechnya, in parts of Central Asia and in the Muslim immigrant communities throughout Europe. The Islamist message can be heard in mosques across Denmark, in the United Kingdom and throughout Europe; it appears on numerous websites, it is available on cassette tape, in pamphlets, on DVD and CD-ROM, and when a number of Danish Islamic groups and organizations host discussions and debates, it is the message that is offered.

A Clash of Civilizations or a Conflict of Interpretation?

One might feel that it is healthy and expressive of a process of confrontation and change that Muslims in the Middle East are voting for Islamists, and that Muslims in European cities are expressing, in speech and writing, their criticism of the Western model of society. The latter must be recognized as an affirmation of one of the most basic rights adhered to in open, Western liberal societies, namely the right to freedom of expression.

It may also be noted that many Islamists and their adherents, likely the vast majority, are not seeking a confrontation with Western nations, neither in nor outside of Europe. But the fact cannot be disregarded that the conflict between those who embrace liberal values and those who want a society based on Islamic values is greater than ever before, and that this conflict on the one hand is fuelled by the war on terror waged by the West, and on the other hand by terrorism in and outside of Western societies carried out by militant Islamists. It seems undeniable that the American political scientist Samuel Huntington was right when in 1993 he predicted that the next major global conflict would consist in a clash of civilizations.[2] Huntington's use of the inadequately defined concept of 'civilization' was the main cause of widespread criticism and disapproval of his theory in academic circles and among liberal thinkers. The main problem with Huntington's theory – though not as clear cut an issue as it has often been claimed – is that it can yield the impression that civilization is an entirely stable and ahistorical phenomenon, which is based in religion and is therefore trapped in a narrow frame of interpretation based on simple, and simplistic, dogma.

But this is exactly how religion is understood by fundamentalists: as a narrow, fixed and dogmatic interpretation or understanding, which explains everything and outline how the true, good and beautiful life must be lived. As such, fundamentalism opposes change, the kind of change to which societies and civilizations are always subject.[3] This change requires that religious values must be reinterpreted in order to adjust to the historical changes which societies necessarily undergo. This is true for Islamic history as well as for Christian history, and within both traditions reinterpretations have met with fundamentalist reaction. This battle over the significance of values both indicates and contributes to the process of change within religions as well as civilizations; therefore, by its nature of being submerged in the maelstrom of history, the substance of these is constantly up for debate. As a part of this process, communities form over particular construals of values, including religious meanings. Such communities of interpretation exist on many levels.[4] On one level, the Danish Evangelical Lutheran Church constitutes an example of a community based on an interpretation of Christian values within an Evangelical-Lutheran tradition, while at the same time smaller communities of interpretation, such as Grundtvigians and Inner Mission Evangelicals, exist on a different level; the groups, while belonging to the community of the Danish Evangelical Lutheran Church, hold differing views on certain issues. These groups nevertheless have more in common with each other, as far as their understanding of Christianity is concerned, than any of them do with the Catholic Church. But this, too, may be subject to change, as a case in point.

Fundamentalist opposition to change is most evident in the view that basic values cannot be interpreted: referring to eternal and unalterable truths, they monopolize interpretation and are at times willing to resort to violence in an effort to maintain this monopoly, as when pro-life activists in the United States bomb medical clinics because they consider the work done there to be in violation of God's commandments.

Huntington's prediction that the next major global conflict would consist in a clash of civilizations was correct, provided that we understand this as a battle between different understandings of which values should serve as the basis for both global and regional order, for instance in the Middle East. We find ourselves in the midst of a global battle over values, in the overall shape of a battle between one community of interpretation, Islamism, which prioritizes Islamic law in the establishment of order, and another community of interpretation, that of liberal humanism, of which George W. Bush appears as self-appointed head exegete, and which considers individual civil liberties to be essential prerequisites for order, security and stability. The Islamist community of interpretation is, however, clearly not identical with the Islamic civilization, just as no identity exists between the liberal-humanist community of interpretation and Western civilization: many Muslims who belong to the Islamic civilization, including many in Western societies, adhere to Islam as part of their everyday lives while also embracing the values of liberal humanism, just as it is not uncommon for people within Western civilization to be highly critical of liberal democracy.

Islamism

The Islamist opposition, which is most potently expressed in militant insurrection and terrorism, is by no means a novel phenomenon. Neither is it directed solely at Western liberal values and the Western adherence to constitutional democracy as the best means of securing social order. It is also directed at secular, authoritarian Arab regimes, even at the Saudi Arabian government, which, in accordance with the way in which it understands and presents itself, legitimizes its supremacy by referring to its foundation in Islamic orthodoxy. Saudi Arabia can be seen as exemplifying the Islamist battle over values: after the First World War, the state of Saudi Arabia was founded on the twin strengths of the sword and a particular interpretation of Islam. This particular interpretation is attributed to the Islamic reformer Muhammad bin Abd al-Wahhab (1703-1792), and accordingly named *Wahhabism*. It constitutes a fundamentalist interpretation of the Koran and the canonized texts.[5]

According to this interpretation, being a good Muslim entails strict compliance with prescripts, extracted from the Holy Scriptures and the life of the Prophet Muhammad, concerning the right conduct of life and the way in which society must be structured. These prescripts also, as a matter of principle, constitute the only true law of the community. Allah is the only true sovereign; all people and societies must submit to his law, as it is revealed in the Koran. Under this interpretation, democracy, under which the people (demos) are sovereign and lawmakers both, is indeed blasphemous, at least according to those living within the Wahhabi social order, which is the case – or, at least in their own understanding, should be the case – in Saudi Arabia. But this very issue spawns the internal conflict which has threatened the independent Saudi Arabian state since its inception in 1932. Its borders were primarily determined by the British, who sought to further their own interests in the Middle East. The same was the case in Kuwait and Iraq. Here, the Wahhabist order, under the leadership of the House of Saud, came up against boundaries determined by the necessities of *realpolitik*. The vanguard of the House of Saud, the so-called Brotherhood (Ikhwan), who were sent to fight the tribes and include them under the new order, refused to accept this boundary determined by *realpolitik*. Their ultimate objective was to reinstate the Islamic order in all of the former Ottoman Empire, from Turkey through Iraq and the Arabian Peninsula to the Near East and Northern Africa. This vision of the resurrection of the *Caliphate* (derived from *Caliph*, successor, namely to the Prophet Muhammad) was not compatible with the interests of the European powers, and expansion towards the North and East was therefore halted at the so-called Trucial States (the small Gulf states) and Iraq, and at Transjordania to the West; a fact which king Abd al-Aziz ibn Abd al-Rahman al-Saud (Ibn Saud, 1856-1953) had to accept due to circumstances of *realpolitik*.[6] In the final stages of the process of consolidating his new order, he was therefore forced to neutralize and oppress his own foot soldiers after their mission had been completed. Although they wish to employ different means in order to achieve it, the shared objective of Islamists in European societies and Jihadists in the Middle East may appropriately be described as *pan-Islamic nationalism*, meaning the utopian notion of the resurrection of the Caliphate.

This clash between the necessities of practical politics (state formation) and idealist vision (legitimacy) remains an internal threat to the stability of the Saudi Arabian order. The Islamist opposition rests upon the shoulders of noble forebears possessing a pure and immaculate interpretation of Islam, from which stem the notions of *Salafi* and *Salafism* (the followers of the predecessors, or early generations, of Islam, including sheik Wahhab). They judge every aspect of the performance of the Saudi Arabian government on the basis of its own postulated foundation of legitimacy, and are critical of the government's yielding to the demands of practical politics, which is leading Saudi Arabia still further away from the true path of Islam.[7] For the Salafists in Saudi Arabia, then, the royal family in Riyadh constitutes the enemy close at hand, while the United States and the infidel West, with which the royal family is allied – whether due solely to the necessities of *realpolitik* or also due to the fact that it enjoys the consumer goods on offer in affluent Western societies – constitute the more distant enemy.

In Egypt, a different yet analogous development has taken place. The British presence in the Nile country came to an end when the Islamic fundamentalists of the Muslim Brotherhood, which had been established in the late 1920's, assisted in bringing Gamal Abd al Nasser (1918 – 1970) to power.[8] The Egyptian Islamists had thus exhausted the purpose Nasser needed them to serve, and he proceeded to do his utmost to have them removed from the Egyptian political scene, by banning their organization and imprisoning their leaders. Nevertheless, the ideology of the Muslim Brotherhood spread throughout the Middle East, where it now constitutes the basis for a transnational Islamist opposition – a pan-Islamic nationalism. In spite of the fact that it is still banned there, in Egypt where some members are allowed to participate in the political process as independent politicians the Brotherhood presently represents the most serious challenge to the current regime led by Hosni Mubarak. Some of the Muslim brothers ended up in Saudi Arabia. In the community surrounding the Muslim centers of learning in Mecca they got together with the Salafists and developed a synthesis of the Egyptian and the Saudi Islamist ideology.[9] Osama bin Laden, a Saudi Arabian, and his ideological and strategic ally Ayman al-Zawahiri, an Egyptian, emerge as the personification of this synthesis.

Obviously, a number of other versions of Islamism exist, such as the Shia Muslim interpretation attributable to Ayatollah Khomeini, which became the ideological basis for the Iranian revolution of 1979, making Iran an Islamic republic. Other versions are characteristic of the regions and contexts within which they have developed, for instance in North Africa, Pakistan and South East Asia. As I have already implied, Islamism is a *political ideology* which, based in a fundamentalist interpretation of Islam, is endeavoring to introduce a particular societal order; an order based on the Islamist understanding of which values should form the basis for a society. Such an interpretation always emerges from a specific context, never out of a vacuum. Islamism as such must therefore remain an abstract and generalized concept. In the same sense, there are numerous ways in which a societal order based on liberal and democratic values can be realized. Specific contexts produce communities of interpretation, and within these they define themselves, through a delimitation in relation to that which they are not. The battle over values which is currently taking place in the Middle East therefore not only represents a conflict between Islamism and liberal-humanist values. It is also significantly representative of a struggle between Muslims to determine the true nature of Islam, and how their societies should be ordered. This alone is enough to render any talk of a clash of civilizations in terms of a conflict between the West and Islam nonsensical. For under this same heading numerous other struggles subsist, as illustrated most obviously and disconcertingly by the current situation in Iraq, a country which seems to be on the verge of a civil war between a number of different Islamist and nationalist factions.

Madonna, Schiffer, and Rushdie

The war on terror is first and foremost a battle over values. It is a moral struggle to propagate the values on which the Western order is based. George W. Bush has made this clear time and time again, and for this reason this particular war will not be won until the Middle East has become a region of democratic states. But achieving this object will not serve to end the war on terror, for the battle over values is also played out in Central Asia, South Asia, South East Asia, Africa, and in

Western societies. The war on terror may turn out to be a protracted one. As such it is reminiscent of the endless wars of religion – battles over values – waged between Catholics and Protestants for centuries after the collapse of the medieval Christian monoculture in Europe. Only with the 1648 Peace of Westphalia, according to which war could no longer legitimately be waged on the basis of conflicting values, a new era in European history began in which war was regulated and limited, though not abolished. The war on terror is the Thirty Years' War of the 21st century. It is a war fought on many fronts in a global theater of war.

The Muhammad drawings must be considered in this context. While *Jyllands-Posten,* the government, and probably a majority of Danes thought this incident concerned the Danish battle over values, imams residing in Denmark, ambassadors of Middle Eastern countries, Islamic scholars in the Middle East, and Middle Eastern governments had a different agenda. The incident was exploitable in the battle over values which lies at the heart of the war on terror, in which Denmark takes part. These are the circumstances under which the matter was able to develop in the way it did.

However, this was not the first time a conflict arose because some took offense at a perceived slight of their religion. In 1989 Madonna produced a music video, *Like a Prayer*, which mixed aspects of religion, sex, and race. The video was intended to launch her new record, which it certainly did: the record became a smash hit, receiving rave reviews which proclaimed it an artistic breakthrough. But Christian America and the Cardinals of the Vatican were outraged, and according to a *USA Today* guest column authored by the head of the American Family Association, Donald Wildmon, the "video … is an extension of a disturbing trend by some in the media, that of disrespect and disdain for the religious beliefs of millions of Americans."[10] In particular, Christians took exception to Madonna's make-up suggestive of stigmata – wounds inflicted upon Jesus' hands when he was nailed to the cross – and to the burning crosses shown in the background at the end of the video. Madonna, a devout Catholic who used to pray with her staff before concerts, expressed a different opinion: "I was exorcising the Catholic Church feelings of guilt about sex and masturbation."[11] She achieved record sales, but had to cancel two concerts in Italy, and lost a Pepsi sponsorship deal: the company chose to apologize to customers in an effort to avoid a spreading boycott of Pepsi products. As the discussion in Part 1 of this book will show, the United States hesitated to respond to the Muhammad cartoon controversy. The Madonna incident, however, shows that, on the subject of religion, Americans, much like the Catholics in Rome and the Muslims, may hold rather ambivalent views concerning freedom of expression and aesthetic creativity when religion is involved. Indeed, this may account for the hesitant American response to the Muhammad cartoon issue.

Another example was the Karl Lagerfeld dress worn by supermodel Claudia Schiffer at a January 1994 Chanel fashion show in Paris. The dress, which barely covered her ample bosom, featured Arabic calligraphy which turned out to be a well known verse from the Koran. An outraged Muslim world responded with fatwas against Schiffer and Lagerfeld, and threats of a boycott against Chanel products.[12] The standard bearers in the campaign against Schiffer's dress were the Indonesian *Muslim Scholars Council* in Jakarta. Saudi Arabian newspapers fully covered the controversy, but also covered accompanying pictures in black ink. The Saudi Arabian public had to do without Ms. Shiffer's bare shoulders, cleavage, or stockinged legs. In this case, as in the cases of the Muhammad drawings and Salman Rushdie's *Satanic Verses*, a very active role in disseminating the offending material was played by the very people who took offense. In all three cases the offended parties took pains to ensure that the offenses were turned into scandals and media events. Reacting to the controversy, which by then had forced Claudia Schiffer to hire a bodyguard, Karl Lagerfeld explained that he had found the verse in a book on the Taj Mahal and had taken it for a love poem. Lagerfeld and Chanel issued apologies as well as an assurance that the dress itself as well as all sketches, photos and prints of the dress had been burned. With allegedly 70 per cent of Chanel's exports going to Saudi Arabia Chanel chose profits over artistic freedom, which is unsurprising given that the *raison d'etre* of any company is to make a profit.

Prior to the case of the Muhammad drawings, the Rushdie affair had shown how dramatic such a matter could become. On February 14, 1989 Ayatollah Khomeini, the religious leader of Iran, issued a *fatwa* calling for the death of Salman Rushdie for blaspheming against Islam in his

The Battle over Values

Death threats were issued against Claudia Schiffer for her perceived offense against Islam following her 1994 modeling of a dress adorned with a verse from the Koran, designed by Karl Lagerfeld for Chanel.

novel *The Satanic Verses*. Rushdie based his novel on a traditional story, known to Islamic tradition as well as to the European interpretation of Islam, according to which the Prophet Muhammad at one point inserted into the Koran a verse describing three goddesses by the names of al-Lat, al-Uzza and Manat, who were the daughters of Allah, and were able to intercede with Allah on one's behalf. This verse was supposedly added for political reasons, in order to attract more converts to Islam from among the population of Mecca, where the three goddesses were said to be very popular. The Archangel Gabriel appeared before Muhammad to reproach him for the verse: Allah had no issue, and most certainly no daughters! The revelation about the three goddesses was the work of Satan. The verses were removed with the words "but God erases what Satan inserts." Islamic tradition dismisses this story as inauthentic, while by the enemies of Islam it can be used to challenge the principles of the unity of God and the status of the Koran as an unedited revelation. Rushdie in fact challenges the latter principle in his novel, which also features a number of controversial passages which reflect badly on the Prophet and on Islam.[13]

The publication of *The Satanic Verses* immediately provoked forceful reactions in the Islamic world. Published on September 26, 1988, it was banned in India by October 5. Within two months it had been banned in Pakistan, Saudi Arabia, Egypt, Somalia, Bangladesh, Sudan, Malaysia, Indonesia, and Qatar. February saw five people shot during demonstrations in Islamabad, and five others shot during a demonstration in Bombay. Demonstrations and book burnings took place in several countries, including the United States. In 1991 the Japanese translator was murdered in Tokyo. Subsequently, 1993 saw Rushdie's Norwegian publisher shot and seriously wounded in Oslo, and thirty-seven dead when local demonstrators set fire to a hotel in Sivas, Turkey, where the Turkish translator was participating in a seminar.

It is worth noting that violent demonstrations only appeared four months after the publication of *The Satanic Verses*. To Rushdie, the banning of the book in India seemed a ploy in the ongoing electoral campaign. In a letter to Rajiv Gandhi, Prime Minister of India 1984-89, Rushdie wrote: "[they] don't really care about my novel one way or the other. The real issue is, who is to get the Muslim vote?," and considering the Indian banning of the novel it is hardly surprising and only barely noteworthy that a number of other countries followed suit, which were hardly renowned for permissiveness and freedom of expression.[14] Much like in the case of the Muhammad drawings, where eleven nations of the Middle East directed their ambassadors to write a letter to Prime Minister Anders Fogh Rasmussen, the Rushdie affair provoked swift governmental action. In both cases, however, a significant amount of time passed before matters took a violent turn, and in both cases local activists contributed to the internationalization of the controversy. It may be of interest, then, to consider the common features of the two cases.

The Rushdie affair began in the United Kingdom. Here, longstanding tension persists between Muslim immigrants and the native population. Muslim unemployment was high, they were hit particularly hard by tax reform, and unlike the Jewish and Catholic minorities, Muslims were not granted governmental subsidies for their own schools. Feminist criticism of third-world family patterns was primarily aimed at Muslims, and much was made of the fact that the British legal system only recognizes blasphemy against Christianity.[15] Muslim attempts at drawing political attention to these problems, and other effort to better conditions had not only failed but were largely ignored. As a result, discontent blossomed in areas with large Muslim communities such as Bradford. Moderate protests soon developed into radical demands for the novel to be recalled and for compensatory financial contributions to Muslim charities. Three and a half months after the publication of *The Satanic Verses* images of the Bradford book burnings were shown around the world, and the violent demonstrations were portrayed as spontaneous acts by radical Muslims. In truth, this was a carefully orchestrated campaign. Prior to the demonstrations, pages from the book had been photocopied and distributed among would-be protestors and duly notified journalists, in order to ensure maximum coverage and understanding of the issues. The campaign was financed by groups in Pakistan and Saudi Arabia competing for influence among Muslim immigrants in the United Kingdom. Though this arrangement made a strong impression the world over, the book burnings were most likely an expression of social discontent rather than outrage caused by a book nobody had read.

Another month passed before Khomeini issued a fatwa. That this was a highly political act is illustrated by the fact that *The Satanic Verses* had actually been reviewed in Iran, sparking no unrest whatsoever. His earlier works, *Shame* and *Midnight's Children*, were well-known in Iran, the former even receiving an award for best translation into Persian. This award was presented by none other than the then-president and current religious leader of Iran, the successor to Ayatollah Khomeini, Ali Khamenei. On March 10, 1989, Khamenei told the *Iran Times*, "anyone intending to publish a similar book or adapt it for the screen, show it in a movie theater – from this point on they will each face the risk of getting killed by Muslims."[16]

In an interesting indication of an internal power struggle in Iran over the correct interpretation of Islam, within days of Khomeini's fatwa being issued Ali Khamenei called for Rushdie to publicly apologize for his actions, as part of an effort to resolve the matter diplomatically. This suggestion was favorably received by a British government whose response to Khomeini's fatwa had been vague and hesitant, and which was eager to find a diplomatic solution to the long-standing diplomatic incident between Iran and the United Kingdom. Though the Iranian occupation of the American Embassy in 1979-81 had led to a very frosty relationship between Iran and the United Kingdom, in the year leading up to the Rushdie affair the two countries had sought a rapprochement. Both governments were apparently interested in ensuring that the temperature of their new relationship did not plummet because of a novel. Five days after the issuance of the fatwa Rushdie did in fact issue an apology – or rather, he issued a statement of regret curiously similar to that issued by *Jyllands-Posten* in a response to the cartoon controversy: "as author of *The Satanic Verses* I recognize that Moslems in many parts of the world are genuinely distressed by the publication of my novel. I profoundly regret the distress that publication has occasioned to the sincere followers of Islam. Living as we do in a world of many faiths this experience has served to remind us that we must all be conscious of the sensibilities of others."[17] Tehran immediately rejected this apology, and confirmed the death sentence.

The overwhelming power wielded by Iranian religious leaders is characteristic of the relationship between politics and religion in Iran. This is borne out by the Rushdie affair. In 1989 Khomeini was concerned that the Islamic revolution was losing momentum: the previous year had seen an armistice with Iraq, Iran enjoyed only limited success in exporting the revolution to the wider Middle East, and in Afghanistan, the Mujahedeen, aided by Sunni Muslims and the Americans, had achieved a prestigious victory against the Soviet Union. Khomeini's ambitions of exporting the revolution to the wider Islamic world, thereby making his Islamic doctrine central for Muslims throughout the world, was opposed by powerful forces in Iran who, after the devastating war with Iraq, sought to nationalize the revolution. This would have amounted to conducting a pragmatic foreign policy in order to ensure the country's return to the international community. Vehemently opposed to this policy of reconciliation, Khomeini used the fatwa to put himself and his Islamist policies at the top of the international agenda once more, and he had the sheer audacity to extend the authority of the fatwa beyond the house of Islam, including the Western world. In other words, with this fatwa, the Islamist strategy for the resurrection of the Caliphate went from being the concern of the Islamic world to constituting a global battle over values. The Rushdie affair, the controversy over Claudia Schiffer's dress as well as the far more serious cartoon controversy must be seen in this light. They are indicative of the struggle to determine which world order will achieve dominance.

European governments were astounded and outraged by Khomeini's fatwa. A hesitant British government initially opted to simply observe developments. At the February 20 meeting of the European Council several of the twelve EEC countries, led by West Germany and France, pressed for a more forceful response than a mere condemnation of the fatwa and Iran. The United Kingdom followed suit. Recalling all ambassadors to Iran, the twelve EEC countries issued an unequivocal statement asserting that under no circumstance would relations with Iran be normalized unless the Iranian government unconditionally distanced itself from the fatwa, which to European ministers constituted a clear violation of state sovereignty. Despite the unequivocal nature of these demands, the EEC ambassadors returned to Tehran within a month, although no action had been taken by Iran, other than their confirmation of the fatwa. With some justification the Iranian Minister of Foreign Affairs was able to comment rather triumphantly that "Islam had forced the EEC back to reality." Within a few months European cooperation in this matter crumbled, and in the years 1989-1992 individual countries, including Denmark, strengthened their bilateral ties with Iran.[18]

The policy of the EEC countries towards Iran was inconsistent for a number of reasons. The Hezbollah, supported by Iran, was still detaining European hostages in Beirut, and negotiations with Iran were necessary to ensure their release. In spite of its strongly voiced demands at the meeting of the European Council in February, West Germany (which became the reunited Germany shortly afterwards) was eager to maintain a cordial relationship with Iran. Paraphrasing Shakespeare, one might say that the German bluster was a case of much ado about nothing; the German resolve soon crumbled, and this also adequately describes the EEC countries' policies towards Iran, until a decision was made at the 1992 European Council meeting in Edinburgh to initiate a 'critical dialogue' with Iran. Their significant economic interests in Iran were another reason for the EEC countries' inconsistent policies towards Iran and the fatwa.[19] An additional influence on EEC policies regarding the fatwa was Iran's pragmatic and constructive approach to efforts to dislodge Iraqi forces from Kuwait following the invasion in August of 1990, which came as a pleasant surprise to European, Middle Eastern, and American politicians. However, in this matter Iranian efforts at cooperation with the UN and Western countries were due to the regime's hostility towards Saddam Hussein's regime, rather than to a veneration of Western democracies. The fatwa remained a major stumbling block for a normalization of EU-Iran relations. To the United States this was but one more reason for maintaining the politics of confrontation with Iran. During the Clinton administration this adversarial relationship became further entrenched, with the United States instigating sanctions against Iran in 1993, 1995, and 1996. The Europeans instead sought a pragmatic solution which would allow Iran to return to the fold through dialogue. Demands for political reform, improvements in the field of human rights, and a disassociation from Khomeini's fatwa were accompanied by promises of economic cooperation and European investments in Iran, whose energy sector in particular was in need of modernization. With the 1997 election of reformist Muhammed Khatami, who initiated a program of *Dialogue between Civilizations*, a pragmatic solution presented itself, whereby Iran agreed not to follow through on the death sentence issued by Khomeini while the Europeans turned a blind eye to the activities of Tehran clerics who continued to affirm the validity of the fatwa, and to the price on Rushdie's head which rose year by year.

Western governments chose to take the fatwa very seriously because they feared that the powerful ideological leader of Iran might conceivably direct the powerful network of agents under his command to carry out the fatwa. Adding to this worry was the fact that Iranian operatives had carried out missions in other countries before, orchestrating the murder of dissidents. In order to add weight to the Ayatollah's proclamations the *15 Khordan Foundation* announced a reward to the person or persons who killed Rushdie. The reward, as accompanied by an exhortation to carry out the fatwa, is still claimable and the amount of money has increased every year since 1989. In 2005 it was $2.8 million. It is important to understand that a fatwa is not a governmental announcement which can be altered or annulled at a later date. It is an assessment by an Islamic scholar which one may choose to comply with or ignore. The only way for the fatwa to be annulled would be for Khomeini or his successor, Khamenei, to give a different assessment. For instance, they might announce that it is contrary to Islamic law to kill an author, such as Salman Rushdie. However, according to Islamic tradition the first fatwa would probably not have been void, and in any case a second fatwa has not been issued. To the contrary, Khamenei announced on January 19, 2005, that he still feels that Rushdie deserves to die. At a 1999 meeting of the UN General Assembly the Iranian government announced that it would not actively carry out the fatwa, which in turn led to mutual accreditation of ambassadors between Iran and the United Kingdom. Yet the religious leaders, who hold the reigns of power in Iran, have made clear their opposition to this policy time and time again, most recently in a statement issued on January 14, 2006 by the governmental news service IRNA: "the fatwa is irrevocable." It must be a cause of worry to Salman Rushdie that the most vocal proponents of the validity of the fatwa are intimate associates of the Iranian Revolutionary Guard, as this very same Guard is the foundation of power for President Mahmoud Ahmedinejad, who was elected in 2005. Though Western governments now pragmatically *consider* the matter closed for political reasons, the Rushdie affair has not been concluded these seventeen years after the Ayatollah Khomeini pronounced the death sentence.

There are some interesting similarities between the Rushdie affair and the Muhammad cartoon controversy. Both cases saw Muslim reaction on two levels, the governmental and the international. Both cases saw early attempts on the part of governments to contain the problem before it got out of hand. When India and number of other countries banned *The Satanic Verses* they were probably not acting out of concern for Salman Rushdie or Western countries, but rather in an attempt to avoid a confrontation with the Islamists. The eleven Muslim ambassadors' demarche to the Danish Prime Minister can be interpreted in this way as well: as an effort to prevent the hijacking of the matter by Islamist opposition groups. Although the Prime Minister declined the meeting, the Danish government did seek to handle the matter through diplomatic channels, as was the British strategy in the Rushdie affair. The Danish Ministry of Foreign Affairs worked with connections such as the Organization of the Islamic Conference (OIC) and the Arab League. It remains an open question whether a meeting between Prime Minister Anders Fogh Rasmussen and the eleven ambassadors in October of 2005 could have changed the course of events. It is obvious that the British attempt at a diplomatic solution

In 1996 Denmark landed its own Rushdie affair when Prime Minister Poul Nyrup Rasmussen called off the Aristeion Award ceremony intended to honor Rushdie for his latest book, The Moor's Last Sigh, *on the grounds that Denmark could not ensure his safety. After a turbulent month that almost saw the fall of the Danish government, Rushdie came to Denmark to accept the award. Bowing to the demands of its parliamentary opposition, the government survived by pledging support for democratic opposition groups in Iran.*

failed, and that Rushdie's statement of regret only served to make him seem less credible. In both cases the conflict escalated when influential imams began calling for action, encouraged by campaigns launched by angry Muslims in Denmark and the United Kingdom, respectively. The large demonstrations against *The Satanic Verses* took place in Pakistan and India only after the book burnings had taken place in Bradford, and similarly, imams in Cairo, Mecca, and on satellite television only made the decision to call for demonstrations and a boycott of Danish goods after angry Danish Muslims, working with the Egyptian Embassy in Copenhagen, brought news of the cartoon incident to the Middle East. In turn, Middle Eastern governments were forced to address the issue. Both cases were politicized by angry Muslims in Denmark and the United Kingdom who felt discriminated against, and who were able to relate this feeling of discrimination to an international battle over values being fought among Muslims in the Middle East as well as between the Islam world and the West. Exactly how this was possible is unclear, but the fact that it *was* possible indicates that these cases, once exposed, were ideally suited for a political mobilization of Muslims in the global battle over values.

Islamism and Order

The Islamist battle over values is primarily a struggle within Islamic countries to determine which interpretation of Islam should form the basis for the reigning social order. Three overall construals of the relationship between Islam and politics can be identified. First, the order of Khomeini and the Salafists, under which politics is completely subordinated to Islam, meaning that a fundamentalist interpretation of Islam constitutes the decisive and pervading principle governing the construction of social order: *The Islamist Order*. Secondly, the order of the founder of modern Turkey, Kemal Atatürk, under which Islam is completely subordinate to politics, that is to say, a forced secularization under which all religious symbols are banned from public life: *The Kemalist Order*. Thirdly, an order under which Islam and politics are in balance. Under this system, religion is adjusted to a political system based on the fundamental values of the UN Universal Declaration of Human Rights. The first order embraces the Islamization of the state, the second order subsumes Islam in the state, while referring religion entirely to the private sphere, and the third order makes religion a societal matter, so that religion may serve as an intermediary between the individual and the state, as is the case in many European countries: *The Secular Order*.

The struggle to determine which order will prevail in the countries of the Middle East has been going on for a long time. The Western powers begat the Middle Eastern system of states at the end of the First World War, and the West has been party to this struggle ever since. As clearly shown by the Iranian revolution, the terrorist activities of al-Qaida, Syria's 1982 massacre of the Muslim Brotherhood, the internal conflict in Saudi Arabia, and the civil war in Algeria, this struggle tends to turn violent and bloody. Since the Middle Eastern states achieved independence, the West has taken three distinct approaches to this battle over values: during the Cold War the West completely ignored the battle over values in the interest of maintaining the balance of power. Later, Western governments have sought to support the forces for a secular order in the Middle East by means of sanctions and critical dialogue. Most recently, after September 11, the West has sought to initiate a democratic revolution in the Middle East through military intervention.

The first and most dramatic step taken under this new policy towards the Middle East was the war in Iraq, which was intended to launch the project for a new and democratic order in the region. A discussion of the background, course and consequences of the war in Iraq is crucial to understanding the situation in the Middle East today and the battle over values which is fought within that region as well as between Islamists and the West. In Part 1, we will focus on that discussion and on Western policy towards Syria, Palestine, and Iran.

Part 1
Regime Change as Strategy

Where is the mutual agreement or voluntary association so much talked of?

David Hume in *Of the Original Contract*, 1741

Democracy does not work without participation, and participation does not work without influence. The ballot of course provides this influence, but this is not considered to be adequate for modern man. And it should not be adequate, when our concern is that individuals are to have duties as they have rights as well as a greater responsibility for their everyday lives and destinies, in order to go past the atomized and state-supported yet dependent and un-free individual. It is therefore necessary that more must be managed by individuals, families and social networks, however differently they may apply their resources. Over-scrupulous justice constitutes a philosophy of equality which denies differences between individuals. Enabling the implementation of different, yet independently developed, solutions, provides the opportunity to learn from each other rather than from the state. And the individual experiences the usefulness of having opinions and objectives, for oneself and for one's community. This was, after all, the point of Hume's proposed perfect state and the basic idea underlying Burke's notion of letting the colonists govern themselves.

Per Stig Møller in *Den Naturlige Orden (The Natural Order)*, 1996

Democracy as Shock Therapy in the Middle East

George W. Bush drew much attention when, in a November 2003 speech in Washington, he declared that the Western Middle East strategy of the last 60 years had failed because it had sought its goal of stability in the Middle East through cooperation with dictatorships and tyrannies.[20] He reiterated this point at a Whitehall speech during an official visit to London.[21] With a reference to President Woodrow Wilson's declaration of war on Germany in 1917, in which he stated that "the world must be made safe for democracy", Bush declared that peace and security can only be attained through the propagation of freedom and democracy. During the Cold War the United States had allied itself with those Middle Eastern states which sided with the Americans against the Soviet Union. Under this arrangement, these states guaranteed the free flow of oil at a stable price while assuming a pragmatic role in the Israeli-Palestinian conflict. Where these conditions were met, the United States had no qualms about close cooperation, although the states in question were governed without any semblance of democracy or respect for human rights. In this manner the Americans after the Second World War developed a close relationship with Saudi Arabia, a country which is exemplary in terms of the disregard of rights, the absence of democracy, and an enforcement of power which even today comprises public executions, dismemberment and a state of social control bordering on the totalitarian. The intimate cooperation with Saudi Arabia, the other Arab states in the Gulf and Egypt was continued under the Clinton administration in spite of the greater focus on democracy and the values of liberty which characterized the global security policy of that administration.[22]

Clinton's successor, George W. Bush, initially toned down the idealism. During his first presidential campaign, in which he faced Democratic candidate Al Gore, he argued that the United States was not to engage in conflicts around the world, unless interests vital to American security were at stake. The leading advisors on matters of national security policy were Condoleezza Rice, who became national security advisor, and Colin Powell, who assumed control of the State Department during the first George W. Bush administration. Having played key roles during the last phases of the Cold War, they represented a pragmatic security policy focused on the balancing of power.[23] The stage was set for foreign and security policies which would be focused on global power balance issues, with China as a future contender; on the establishment of a missile defense system which entailed increased American unilateralism; and on reducing the commitment of the United States to the state building projects which Clinton had gradually stepped up during his second term in office.

This policy ended with the terrorist attacks on September 11, 2001. An activist foreign policy based on the propagation of freedom and democracy through a confrontational and, if necessary, military strategy was formulated in the *National Security Strategy of the United States* document which was presented to Congress in September 2002.[24] High-profile ideologues in the Bush Administration such as Deputy Secretary of Defense Paul Wolfowitz, Vice President Dick Cheney, and politically appointed senior officials such as Douglas Feith, John Bolton, Richard Perle and David Wurmser contributed significantly to the formulation of the new strategy, which they had been developing in a number of different think tanks since the mid-1990s.[25] They envisioned the road to a stable Middle East, which would guarantee the security of Israel, ensure a stable supply of oil and create reliable partners in the region, as going through a comprehensive reform process, which would result in the democratization of the whole region.

The advantages were obvious. With democratic states in the Middle East a relaxation of tensions would follow, the U.S. would have loyal, dependable partners in the war on terror, and the rising Islamist force, which even before September 11 constituted a threat to the world both in terms of terrorism and the proliferation of weapons of mass destruction would be halted. Iraq was the first major step; Afghanistan constituted merely a necessary distraction for these strategists, one which had to be gotten out of the way as swiftly as possible. *Shock and Awe,* the concept of war which the U.S. developed for the purpose of conquering Iraq, soon gained a more generalized and metaphorical meaning: as a strategy of war, it signified the use of overwhelming military power through massive air bombardments against infrastructural targets combined with an advanced war of information, the purpose of which was to intimidate and shock the Iraqi army and the Iraqi leadership into giving up and deserting.[26] Metaphorically, it meant shaking up the whole region, awakening the forces for democracy by intimidating the Middle Eastern dictatorships and causing their populations to rise up and demand reforms and rights. The velvet revolutions in Eastern Europe which followed the breakdown of the Soviet Union would serve as role models. This meant that the war in Iraq would have to be followed by a purposeful and comprehensive pressure on the regimes in Syria and Iran, while at the same time forces for reform everywhere were to receive support. After the war in Iraq the means applied would be sanctions, diplomatic pressure, threats of military intervention (the seriousness of which, on the part of the U.S., the war clearly proved), in addition to promises of economic cooperation and aid under the condition that the states continued to develop in the right direction. The latter was launched in November 2003 under the name of *The Middle East Partnership Initiative* (MEPI)[27] and must be seen as a part of what the Americans call public diplomacy,[28] meaning the effort to create a framework for dialogue and cooperation through diplomacy, the use of the mass media to spread information about the democratic intentions of the U.S., investments in the private sector and civil society projects.

From Legality to Legitimacy
The activist U.S. foreign and security policies after 9/11, based on the interlinking of security and values, constitutes a decisive break from the U.S. Middle East policy of the Cold War era, under which international security was related to international law, and where states under the UN were considered to be sovereign entities which could only under very special circumstances become subject to military intervention or attack, meaning if they violated international law, and then only on the basis of a mandate from the UN Security Council. In the UN Charter and during the Cold War *sovereignty* was in principle considered to be inviolable, and any violation, such as Iraq's occupation of Kuwait in 1990, legally justified military action. This was exemplified when the UN subsequently authorized a coalition of willing states under U.S. leadership to evict Iraq from the Arab state. On the one hand, then, one country's violation of the sovereignty of another constituted a basis for making war on the aggressor state which was in accordance with international law, regardless of whether the violated party was a liberal and democratic state or a dictatorial regime. On the other hand, there was no *legal* basis within the international system of law for sanction-

ing a war on a sovereign state merely because it was ruled by a military dictatorship, as was the case with the regimes in Syria and Iraq, or by an absolute dynastic monarchy based on theocratic principles as is Saudi Arabia, or by an Islamist dictatorship as is Iran. In exceptional cases the UN Charter allowed for a state or a group of states to initiate a war against another state, namely in cases where said nation constituted a clear and irrefutable threat. In such a case it would be legal to forestall and eliminate the threat by means of a *preemptive* military attack, defined as such in the UN Charter.[29] There is however no basis, according to international law, for carrying out a *preventive* war. Preventive war is not carried out on the basis of a clearly identified threat, but on the basis of the *expectation* that the activities of a given state aim at enabling it to become a future threat to the sovereignty of other states. Were Israel, for example, on the basis of the tension between Iran and the UN over the Iranian nuclear energy program, to act unilaterally in carrying out a military action against the Islamic republic in order to prevent it from enriching uranium which Israel *expects* will be used in the development of nuclear arms, it would be in clear violation of international law. In fact the debate over the basis for starting a war against Iraq in 2003 centered on this very distinction between *preemptive* and *preventive*: arguably, clear evidence that Iraq actually was in possession of a large stockpile of weapons of mass destruction would provide a legal basis for a preemptive war. A preventive war, however, which would prevent the regime of Saddam Hussein from becoming a future threat, had to be considered illegal.

The novel aspect of the U.S. national security strategy presented in 2002 is that the American government reserves the right to carry out preventive wars, irrespective of the fact that they are called 'preemptive' by the Americans and by George W. Bush. In other words: as was the case with the war in Iraq, the U.S. after 9/11 has considerably broadened the definition of the kind of threat which justifies and legitimizes wars of aggression. The United States is fully aware that this reinterpretation, which subsumes preventive into preemptive warfare, is contrary to international law. This is borne out by the fact that the Americans at the same time reserve the right to act unilaterally on matters of war. Preventive and preemptive warfare is thus not motivated and legitimized by reference to international law; rather, it is *morally* based on the defense of the basic values of free societies, defined as civil liberties and rights and democracy, as well as on a strategic objective of propagating these basic values in regions of the world, mainly the Middle East, on the assumption that the spreading of democracy is the best way of achieving global security. This means that, post-9/11, American security strategy cannot and will not be bound by international law, but is, as a matter of principle, bound by the basic values and, consequently, the morality on which the free world bases itself. From the American perspective, then, it is of little or no actual or fundamental importance that the war in Iraq was illegal, to the extent that it was morally defensible, meaning *legitimate*, according to the American point of view; this will be the case when, and only when, Iraq has become a stable liberal and democratic state or, alternatively, a federation of free and liberal republics.

Actually, American presidents and other heads of state have, to the extent that they have possessed the necessary resources, always reserved the right to wage preventive war – in the sense that it was always an option. But, as stated by former Secretary of State Madeline Albright, this change from option to a central aspect of a national security strategy is a new development.[30] The consequences are twofold: first, legality is replaced by legitimacy, meaning the moral objective of security strategy implementation. This is perfectly analogous with the medieval notion of the Just War, which defined war as legitimate and just, meaning morally defensible, on the condition that the war actually brought about incontrovertible improvements of the given state of affairs.[31] Secondly, it follows that sovereignty is no longer considered an attribute of the state, but is rather construed as *the performance of the state as state:* A state is only sovereign if its conduct, domestically as well as internationally, is in accordance with the basic values of the free world. Two sides to the morally based U.S. security strategy emerge: one is the moral prerogative to implement regime change, if necessary by military force, the other is a moral imperative to propagate freedom and democracy. According to the Bush administration, *public diplomacy* and an offensive defense strategy based on the doctrine of preemptive and preventive warfare with the objective of the implementation of a regime change strategy are inter-complementary. In this way, the American strategy in itself provides the basis of legitimacy on which U.S. policy must be judged, namely that the superpower carries out its strategy in accordance with the basic values it wishes to disseminate throughout the rest of the world. This means that as powerful and invincible as the United States may be in terms of military might, the superpower is equally vulnerable to moral criticism, because its legitimacy depends entirely on the construal of the morally Good which it wishes to impart to the world. In the American understanding, the morally Good is freedom and security: both are sorely lacking in the Middle East and South Asia, but because the U.S. wants to introduce the morally Good as a part of the war on terror, locally the project meets with widespread suspicion and mistrust.

The Troublesome Muhammad Drawings

The U.S. has generally been consistent in implementing its policy. Sanctions against Syria have been tightened after the war in Iraq; Iran is confronted through the UN and through co-operation with the EU, the focus of these efforts being the Iranian nuclear energy development program which is suspected to be a move towards the development of nuclear weapons; the Palestinians have been pressured into holding parliamentary elections; legislation enabling financial and political support for democratic opposition movements in Syria and Iran has been passed; and the U.S. has backed reforms and elections in Iraq, the Arab states in the Gulf, Saudi Arabia, and Egypt. While Bush's first term was characterized by military shock therapy in the form of the wars in Afghanistan and particularly in Iraq, the follow-up efforts at *public diplomacy* have taken priority in the second term. This is illustrated by the significant strengthening of the Department of State, which now comprises two of George W. Bush's most valued advisors, Condoleezza Rice as Secretary of State and Karen Hughes, in charge of the administration's *public diplomacy* effort. For the United States, then, the Danish matter of the drawings of the Prophet Muhammad was highly inconvenient, because they were forced to respond to violent attacks on Danish diplomatic offices, and thereby to support Denmark as well as free speech. But the show of support for the small kingdom which insisted upon the right of newspapers to freely publish drawings which are considered offensive by Muslims, and which Islamists were able to use as a means for their mobilization in the West, has obviously not facilitated the efforts to communicate a genuine desire on the part of the United States and the West to engage in a dialogue with the Islamic world. This constitutes a likely explanation for the hesitant and uncertain nature of the American position and statements on the issue. But long before these occurrences, the shock therapy inflicted by the United States and West in an effort to bring about democracy in the Middle East had met with much resistance, and created the basis for the opposition against the U.S. Middle Eastern policy of both Islamists and certain regimes. The effect of the Muhammad drawings was first of all to provide all sorts of political groups with an effective rallying cry, and, secondly, to change the status of Denmark from that of a largely unnoticed coalition partner to an object of Islamist hatred on par with Israel and the United States, if only for a short while.

Iraq: Illusions Shattered

When George W. Bush assumed office 2001, it soon became clear that his Middle Eastern policy agenda was radically different from that of Clinton: Clinton had focused his energies on resolving the Israeli-Palestinian conflict, which in his view constituted the key to establishing a new, stable order in the Middle East, while the problem of Iraq was pushed aside towards the end of the Clinton presidency. Iraq became the very center of attention for Bush.[32] Until June 2003, Bush assumed a passive role in the Palestinian conflict, offering a disengaged and distanced support for the Israeli Prime Minister Ariel Sharon. The Palestinians, represented by Yasser Arafat, were entirely ignored, because he (Arafat), according to the Israeli and American understanding, was immediately responsible for the Palestinian suicide bombings. Bush launched his career in foreign policy in February 2001 by ordering the bombing of Baghdad, on the grounds that China had installed advanced radar equipment which could be used to take down American and British aircraft patrolling the so-called no-fly zones in northern and Southern Iraq. At the same time Bush declared that the U.S. would not hesitate to use military force in the event of threatening behavior on the part of Saddam Hussein.[33] This constituted a radically different message from that of the Clinton administration during its last two years in office.[34] A seemingly rather bewildered president during that period had stood by while Saddam defied UN sanctions, displayed a threatening attitude towards his neighbors, openly transported illegal oil into Turkey and Syria, and was successful in tying up the UN Security Council by pitting the permanent members against each other. A mere three weeks into the Bush presidency dramatic changes in Middle Eastern policy were heralded: the parties to the Israeli-Palestinian conflict were left to their own devices, while the confrontation between Iraq and the United States was about to escalate.

A number of considerations created the context for this re-evaluation of circumstances: firstly, Bush and his advisors had watched Clinton, who had been handed the Oslo Accords by his predecessor George H. W. Bush, squander his prestige on attempts to resolve the conflict only to see it blown to pieces in an outburst of violence only four months before the close of his presidency. Sydney Blumenthal, senior adviser to President Clinton from 1997 to 2001, tellingly sums up the point in a few sentences in his book *The Clinton Wars*: "On January 17, Arafat had his last telephone conversation with President Clinton. He thanked him for all he had done and told him he was 'a great man.' 'The hell I am' said Clinton. 'I'm a colossal failure, and you made me one.'"[35] Since September 13, 1993, when the Oslo Accords were signed in Washington, Clinton had been on the phone to the Middle Eastern parties on a weekly basis, and with seventeen visits with the president at Pennsylvania Avenue, Arafat had been the head of state most frequently received at the White House throughout the Clinton presidency. Especially during his second term in office Clinton had prioritized the effort to move the process along. The eventual failure cannot be attributed to Clinton's personality or commitment. It resulted mainly from the fact that he was not in possession of the political leverage necessary to carry out his intentions. This meant that, up until the last month of his presidency, Clinton limited his efforts to assisting and facilitating the process rather than actually putting pressure on the parties, particularly Israel.[36] Bush saw that Clinton's efforts had been in vain, and accordingly he and his advisors decided that it would be better for the United States to maintain a low profile for a while – which in addition left the leader of the Likud Party, Sharon, who enjoyed much support within Bush's National Security Council, free to handle the conflict as he saw fit.

Secondly, it became obvious to the Bush administration that tensions were mounting in the Persian Gulf: even as Bush took office, American forces in the Gulf region were in a state of high alert. This state had persisted since October 2000, when suicide bombers in a rubber dinghy laden with explosives impacted with the American destroyer USS Cole, which was docked for refueling at Aden in Yemen. Seventeen American crew members died as a result of the attack, and the destroyed ship had to be towed all the way back to the shipyard in Florida. Europeans were preoccupied with the al-Aqsa Intifada and the unusually high oil prices, which caused frenetic hoarding among consumers,[37] and therefore had little attention to spare for the attack on the USS Cole. Americans, however, were in a state of shock: Though attending to the Middle Eastern conflict, the meeting of the G8 and fundraising for the ongoing election campaign kept him busy, Clinton nonetheless found time to attend memorial services in Norfolk, Virginia, and the congressional Committee on Armed Services conducted a hearing to determine how such a thing could happen. The media were awash with stories concerning the trouble in the Gulf, while flags flown at half-staff for ten days reminded people in the streets of Washington that seventeen seamen had been murdered in yet another act of Islamic terrorism. Although no group or individual had assumed responsibility for the attack on the USS Cole, and irrespective of the fact that it bore no resemblance to the al-Qaida attacks on American embassies in East Africa in 1998, political circles in Washington never doubted that the attack was ascribable to Osama bin Laden's organization. Throughout the following months American intelligence agencies intercepted data which indicated increased levels of activity among anti-American Islamic networks, which was why the American deployments in the Gulf area remained in a state of high alert. There was thus no shortage of warnings about terrorist acts aimed at the U.S., or any shortage of attention paid to the mounting tension in the Gulf, in Washington around the time when Bush succeeded Clinton as president.

The Sanctions Paradox
The CIA as well as several other experts had emphasized the mounting problems in the Gulf region and South Asia.[38] Al-Qaida's activities in Afghanistan, Pakistan and Kashmir were cause for concern. So was the fact that, in spite of promises made, no relief seemed to be in sight as far as the tense relationship with Iran was concerned. In addition, there was a growing awareness that the Saudi Arabian state of affairs would in the long run be untenable. Lastly, to critics of Clinton's policy Iraq

constituted a problem which steadily supplied kindling to the bonfire of anti-American sentiment in the region. Theories did exist which suggested that Iraq was involved in international terrorism, and that the regime collaborated with Osama bin Laden;[39] yet the more common understanding was that Iraq's connections with terrorism were mostly indirect and associated with the unfortunate conflict between Saddam Hussein and the UN in which the Iraqi people had become innocent hostages. From the mid-1990s it became increasingly clear that the UN sanctions imposed on Iraq in 1991, in an attempt to disarm the country, were having a devastating effect on the Iraqi people. In the late 1990s it was reported, by the UN's own agencies, that a serious humanitarian disaster was unfolding among the Iraqi people, who suffered from a lack of food, medicine and proper water supplies, and from poor sanitary conditions and pollution. An estimated one million children would perish before reaching the age of five due to the poor conditions, and the general estimate was that around 60,000 people were dying each year as a consequence of the sanctions. Despite the fact that the sanctions had been imposed by the UN and were widely supported, including by Denmark, they were perceived in the Middle East and South Asia as the work mainly of the United States, which therefore constituted the real source of the suffering of the Iraqi people. The American response was that it was within the power of Saddam Hussein alone to end the sanctions, as they would be removed the moment Iraq complied with the conditions of the ceasefire agreement concerning the scrapping of weapons of mass destruction. The U.S. further claimed that Saddam was taking advantage of the sanctions as part of a cynical power game: he was able to utilize the sanctions for the purposes of propaganda, which in turn helped him control his population; they also enabled his accumulation of vast illegal sums of money through massive smuggling operations; lastly, the sanctions provided him with a means of creating dissent within the UN Security Council. On the other hand, Saddam Hussein's argument that it was the United States' management of the Oil for Food program which was causing all the problems was gaining increasing support.[40]

Certainly it had by 2000 become clear that the sanctions were not working as intended: on the one hand, they were neither serving to weaken the power of Saddam Hussein, nor could they force the dictator to cooperate, let alone to allow into the country the new United Nations Monitoring, Verification and Inspection Commission (UNMOVIC), established by Hans Blix as the result of a December 1999 resolution. Only when the situation came to a head in 2002 did the passing of a new resolution (1441) become possible; a resolution which in November 2002, for the first time since November 1998, sent weapons inspectors into Iraq. On the other hand, the controversy over the sanctions led to the complete subversion of the consensus within the UN. In large parts of the Middle East, the U.S. was then left as the sole culprit which insisted on maintaining the ineffectual sanctions, resulting in mounting criticism. The United States was depicted as a power which, in its ambition for oil and domination, oppressed the Iraqi people with no concern for civilian casualties.[41] The construal of 'American Imperialism' was furthermore inspired by the fact that the U.S. maintained 20,000 troops in the Middle East, and furthermore refrained from putting what the Arabs considered to be the necessary amount of pressure on Israel in order to move along the Oslo Accords. In the United States, the political opposition in particular was aware of the untenable nature of the situation. After ordering the December 1998 four-day retaliatory bombing of Iraq, Clinton's strategy became to seek a solution to the conflict within the framework of the United Nations.[42] This led to the above-mentioned December 1999 resolution, which failed to receive backing from Russia, France, and China, who together with Malaysia decided to abstain from voting in the Security Council. As mentioned, the resolution was never implemented due to obstructive interference on the part of Saddam Hussein, something which he managed to get away with because the United States and the United Kingdom had become isolated within the UN.[43]

With no prospect of a diplomatic solution to the problem of Iraq within the framework of the UN, and in the face of the steadily growing threat posed by Islamic terrorist networks in the Persian Gulf which, together with the escalation of the Israeli-Palestinian conflict, fed off the festering sore which the Iraqi problem had become, alternative strategies were germinating in Washington. For years politicians belonging to the so-called neoconservative movement, most prominently Richard Perle and Paul Wolfowitz, had been arguing for what was known as the regime change strategy. There was only one possible solution in sight, namely that Saddam Hussein be removed from power, and three possible scenarios for achieving this were put forth: a secret coup, an assassination, a method which had been approved by Clinton; an open insurrection, by means of which the Iraqi opposition, supported by the United States, assumed power; or an actual military invasion. The first strategy had failed repeatedly. The second, championed by the neoconservative Republicans, was rejected as unrealistic by the military, while support was mounting for the third option.[44]

Simply put, the most obvious way to proceed would have been to lift the sanctions. Several different considerations made this solution unfeasible: firstly, lifting the sanctions would mean that Saddam Hussein's efforts to obstruct the implementation of the UN resolution would be rewarded with victory, which might inspire other dictators and rogue states to disregard international law and scorn any threats of sanctions. In this way the strategy of deterrence would be undermined, which might encourage countries such as North Korea to undauntedly pursue their objective of developing nuclear arms.

Secondly, it was uncertain whether Iraq was in fact already in possession of weapons of mass destruction. Circumstantial evidence indicated that the country was involved in illegal attempts at financing its continuing production by means of illicit oil revenues. This evidence was made more credible by the fact that Iraq stubbornly refused to allow weapons inspectors to carry out their task in the country. Indeed, the suspicion continued to be taken very seriously in the U.S. because of Iraq's refusal to present documentation for the destruction of biological weapons which it claimed to have carried out in the mid-1990s.[45] Up until 1995 UN weapons inspectors had found nothing to indicate that Iraq continued to produce biological weapons after the Gulf War. But after two of Saddam's sons-in-law, both of whom had been prominent figures of the regime, defected to Jordan and revealed to the CIA that they had been in charge of the production of biological weapons, the UN intensified its investigation. Under considerable strain the Iraqis admitted that they had in fact had a program for the development of biological weapons, but claimed that it had been abandoned and the stocks destroyed. They failed, however, to present any documentation for these claims, which meant that while it was known that weapons such as anthrax had indeed been produced, it was unclear what had become of them.

This situation constituted the background for the decisive conflict between Iraq and the UN, which in November 1998 led to the departure of the weapons inspectors from Iraq which was subsequently bombed by the United States and the United Kingdom. When Iraq in December 2002 handed over almost 14,000 pages documenting its innocence, in an attempt to meet the demands of Resolution 1441, the first thing the Americans looked for was proof that the old weapons had been destroyed. But, according to the Americans, Iraq had again failed to deliver the necessary material. Then, in early March 2003, the Iraqis suddenly, during an excavation south of Baghdad, discovered a huge dumping ground for destroyed VX nerve gas and anthrax, which they felt provided the missing documentation. To the Americans, these games did not confirm that Iraq was in fact not in possession of these weapons, rather they proved that the country would not cooperate with the UN on disarmament as required by the ceasefire conditions of 1991 and explicitly repeated in Resolution 1441. The United States considered this in itself to constitute a violation of 1441, which in this case threatened *serious consequences*, something which the Americans understood to mean an authorization of the use of military force. Certainly the suspect Iraqi conduct towards the UN indicated to the Americans that Iraq in fact did have something to hide, which meant that the sanctions could not be lifted until Saddam Hussein had been removed.

Thirdly, besides repeatedly producing weapons of mass destruction, Iraq was also known to have employed them on several occasions. Although no hard and fast evidence existed that Iraq was actually in possession of weapons of mass destruction, the Americans were convinced that – if the sanctions were lifted – Iraq would proceed to push ahead with the production of biological weapons and perhaps shortly be able to resume their nuclear weapons program. One might say that although Iraq may not have constituted a threat to anyone other than its own population, it seemed highly likely to the Americans that, within the near future, the country *would* become a threat. The reality of this presumed future threat was, according to the U.S., indicated by the past. More specifically, it was borne out by the fact that Iraq had used chemical weapons during the war with Iran, as well as in a 1988 attack on Kurdish civilians in northern Iraq. Furthermore, Iraq had on two occasions attacked its neighbors: Iran in 1980 and Kuwait a decade later.

When this behavior was added to Saddam Hussein's irrefutably brutal and cynical oppression of the Iraqi population, an image emerged of an unpredictable – even irrational – dictator, capable of anything.

In this manner, the threat scenario was constructed on the basis of circumstantial evidence, past sins, and the image of a crazed dictator. The reasoning of the Bush Administration thus ran along the following lines: the sanctions should be lifted, because they had led to a humanitarian disaster, because they left the regime unaffected, and because they served to increase the risk of terrorism and the spreading of weapons of mass destruction. However, the sanctions could not be lifted unless the regime of Saddam Hussein was removed, because it already did or very soon would constitute a serious threat. In the Bush administration's final analysis, the only viable course was a morally motivated preventive war.

An Unnecessary War?
France, Russia and China disagreed with this reasoning. They were backed by many other countries, by people all over the world, and by experts, who either believed that Saddam Hussein did not constitute a threat,[46] or that Iraq could at least be contained through a strategy of deterrence. A number of prominent Republicans – such as the former chief of the American forces in the Gulf region, Anthony Zinni, and Brent Scowcroft, National Security Advisor to Gerald Ford and George H. W. Bush[47] – considered the war to be both a high-risk venture which threatened to ignite the region, and an unnecessary one; they argued that Saddam Hussein, according to past experience, basically acted in a rational manner and could therefore be contained by means of a traditional strategy of deterrence, a view exactly opposite to that of the neoconservatives. Two of the most significant theorists on American security policy, neorealists John J. Mearsheimer and Stephen M. Walt, presented the argument with exemplary clarity in the January 2003 issue of *Foreign Policy*. Under the heading 'An Unnecessary War' they reviewed most of the arguments of the neoconservatives. They rejected the arguments put forth by neoconservative associates of Vice President Dick Cheney, Richard Perle and Paul Wolfowitz for viewing Saddam Hussein as a madman, such as the example of Hussein's use of chemical weapons in the war with Iran and against the Kurds in 1988. Mearsheimer and Walt

pointed out that in fact neither the United States nor any other countries had put any pressure on Iraq in order to make the regime *refrain* from using those weapons, the procurement of which had been facilitated in part by the West.[48] They consequently rejected the argument that Saddam Hussein had to be stopped because he on previous occasions had in fact availed himself of weapons of mass destruction, and was therefore likely to do it again. They presented systematic documentation for the claim that the actions of Saddam Hussein could be explained rationally. This was true of the war against Iran in 1980, which was supported by both Western and Arab countries, as well as of the invasion of Kuwait in 1990, at which point highly ambiguous statements made by the U.S. Ambassador to Baghdad might well have given Saddam Hussein the impression that the United States would refrain from reacting to an Iraqi invasion.[49] "Deterrence did not fail in this case; it was never attempted", the two political scientists dryly concluded. Mearsheimer and Walt analyzed several other examples and showed that in every case Saddam Hussein's actions could be seen as quite rational, and from this they concluded that his regime evidently could be affected by the traditional strategy of 'containment and deterrence'. There was thus no reason whatsoever for war.

The clarity and persuasiveness of the argument made by the two neorealists was matched by a perfect absence from their article of any considerations of the consequences for the Iraqi people of 'containment' and sanctions. Their analysis was based solely on an understanding of the international system as a set of relations between states, which abide by well-defined and rationally comprehensible rules of conduct based primarily on military capacity. The analysis of these interactions disregards the societal structures, culture and, to a great extent, the domestic circumstances of individual countries. On the basis of this analysis they might be correct in asserting that Iraq could be contained and deterred from developing and using weapons of mass destruction. The cost of this, however, would have been twofold: it would have been necessary to continue to impose harsh sanctions on Iraq, and a considerable military presence in the Gulf would have had to be maintained; the kind of presence which seems to have been a significant motivating factor for the anti-American sentiment which led to a number of terrorist attacks, such as 9/11. The cost of the sustained containment of Iraq, then, would be the expense of maintaining considerable military forces in the region, the continuation of quarrels with the international community over the legitimacy of continued sanctions against Iraq, and the application of military pressure on Iraq, which would entail weekly bombings of Iraqi targets, as well as an escalating humanitarian disaster ravaging the Iraqi people – while at the same time the U.S. and its allies would increasingly be exposing themselves as targets of terrorism.

The neoconservative reply to the neorealist charge was that the terrorist attacks on 9/11 resulted directly from 60 years of failed American Middle East policy, and that if a future 9/11 was to be prevented, a democratic revolution in the Middle East had to be promoted. This linking of 9/11 with Iraq was predominantly theoretical and philosophical rather than based on empirical fact. This also formed the basis for how intelligence data should be interpreted: when examining dictatorships such as Iraq it was wrong, perhaps even naïve and certainly dangerous, to rely solely upon an empirical, social scientific method, because a dictator such as Saddam Hussein consciously and systematically hid his intentions. Inspired by the much respected, but in some circles also quite controversial, Chicago professor Leo Strauss, Abram N. Shulsky and Gary J. Schmitt argued for the need for an 'esoteric reading' of intelligence: meaning that the analytical method applied to intelligence material had to be *interpreted*, in the same way as any textual analysis requires not only an examination of the 'surface' meaning of the text, but also requires a reading strategy for discovering the 'hidden meaning' of the text.[50] In 2002 Shulsky was made Director of the Office of Special Plans in the Pentagon, which was charged with evaluating the large influx of intelligence reports on Iraq flowing from the various intelligence agencies of the United States, reports which were often mutually contradictory. Shulsky had previously been affiliated with the influential think tank *RAND Corporation*, while Gary J. Schmitt had been employed by the Senate Select Committee on Intelligence during the Reagan Administration. Both Shulsky and Schmitt were part of the neoconservative milieu in Washington, centered on the think tanks *American Enterprise Institute* and *Project for a New American Century*. As a kind of *avant la lettre* commentary on Mearsheimer and Walt, Schmitt and Shulsky, in their critical article on the use of empirically based social scientific methodology by the intelligence agencies, concluded that, "with the end of the Cold War, the struggle of ideologies has come to a close. Some have foreseen an 'end of history,' in the Hegelian sense of the attainment of philosophic self-awareness; others, a 'clash of civilizations,' in the sense of the conflict of what are ultimately mutually incompatible value systems. For those brought up in the realist tradition, it will seem strange that theories of international relations should have such philosophic origins and implications. Nevertheless, such is the world we face; and the study of the classics of political philosophy with Leo Strauss was a surprisingly good preparation for grappling with it."[51] Speculative philosophy was to replace empiricism.

A Necessary War?
For the United States and the United Kingdom, the main issue was that in the interest of national security the sanctions had to be lifted, but that this, on the grounds of the three previously mentioned concerns, could only happen after the removal of the regime of Saddam Hussein. Opposing this view were countries such as France, Russia and Germany (the latter was about to take over the presidency of the UN Security Council on January 1, 2002). These three nations uniformly claimed that none of the resolutions of the Security Council authorized the execution of a regime change in Iraq by the UN or by the United States. For the UN to approve any military action against Iraq, the country would have to constitute a serious threat against UN member states.

This forced the United States and the United Kingdom to present evidence of an Iraqi program for the development of weapons of mass destruction. The evidence was supplied by a number of reports produced by the CIA, the Pentagon's own intelligence agency, and the threat assessments issued by Tony Blair's office.[52] The reports were backed by analyses issued by several American and British think tanks, but were strongly challenged by skeptics. They pointed out that the material contained no new information, and that the massive body of information presented no conclusive evidence. In one case it could actually be proved that material issued by the office of Tony Blair had been falsified, as parts of an intelligence report turned out to have been copied from a student paper submitted at the Monterey Institute in California.[53] Furthermore, notwithstanding the intelligence supplied to them by the United States, weapons inspectors led by Hans Blix found but a few pieces of circumstantial evidence of the production of weapons of mass destruction.[54] Neither were skeptics convinced by Colin Powell's presentation of evidence to the UN Security Council on February 5, 2003. The speech given by the American Secretary of State failed to demonstrate conclusively that a close collaboration existed between Saddam Hussein's Iraq and Osama bin Laden's al-Qaida network.[55]

This state of affairs made it impossible for the UN Security Council to reach an agreement which would authorize the removal of Saddam Hussein from power by means of military force by a 'coalition of the willing.' This disunity was then willfully ignored by the United States, the United Kingdom and a number of other countries, including Australia, Poland and Denmark, who would go to war in Iraq *sans* mandate. Although some disagreement persists over whether military action arguably was in accordance with UN statutes, independent experts on international law generally agree that there was in fact *no* legal basis for the war.[56] Had the occupying forces in Iraq been able to establish that Iraq had in fact produced weapons of mass destruction, for instance by discovering stockpiles of such illegal weapons, production facilities for them or documents proving their existence, a *post bellum* argument could have been made for the legitimacy of the war, because it would have been shown that Saddam Hussein had in fact posed a real threat. After the war, neither evidence of weapons production nor any connection to al-Qaida was found. This increased the pressure on the governments involved in the war effort – not least that of Tony Blair, who had been accused by critics within his own party of misleading the British people as well as Parliament.

Why War?
Before, during and after the war the above mentioned considerations developed into speculations about other possible reasons the United States might have had for going to war, apart from the objective of disarming the regime of Saddam Hussein. Detractors of the American policy towards Iraq have emphasized the notion that the United States was primarily interested in Iraqi oil resources, and Danish European Commissioner Poul Nielson[57] went as far as to accuse the United States of aspiring to OPEC membership. Attention was drawn to the fact that while war had been waged in Iraq in spite of the absence of conclusive

evidence concerning that country's weapons, no military action was taken against North Korea, which openly admitted to possessing nuclear weapons. According to critics of the Iraq war the decisive difference between the impoverished North Korea and the potentially affluent Iraq was oil. Although the motives of the United states for going to war in Iraq were mainly strategic and ideological, the fact that two-thirds of the world's known oil reserves are in fact located in the Gulf area constitutes an important motivating factor in terms of America's national security interest in the region. Since the Second World War the global economy has been based on the free shipping of oil at stable prices. Every president since Eisenhower has reiterated his 1957 Special Message to Congress, in which he declared that the United States has a vital interest in the region which will be defended with military means if necessary. Henry Kissinger famously proclaimed that "he who controls the Gulf oil reserves has the rest of the world in a stranglehold." Another reason of at least equal importance for the urgent American Cold War interest in the Gulf region was the attempt to keep the Soviet Union away from the region's open harbors, which could provide the Communist great power with unhindered access to the world seas. Also, the very notion that the Soviets might gain control of the oil reserves was anathema to the Americans.

The George W. Bush administration had three strategic reasons for removing Saddam Hussein by military force: Firstly, in spite of the absence of concrete evidence, the Administration remained convinced that Iraq held and produced weapons of mass destruction and was, as part of these efforts, trying to develop nuclear weapons. Secondly, Iraq supported global terrorism, including al-Qaida and Palestinian groups. These were the two reasons presented by then Secretary of State Colin Powell to the UN Security Council in February 2003. Thirdly, Saddam Hussein terrorized his own population; his was a brutal dictatorship, where murder, including mass murder, ethnic cleansing, and the use of weapons of mass destruction were the order of the day

The removal by means of military force of Saddam Hussein would, according to the neoconservatives, not only eliminate a serious threat, it would also liberate the Iraqi people and transform Iraq from being America's major problem in the Middle East to being a useful partner and ally. On the one hand, the ineffectual system of sanctions caused tensions in the Gulf to grow, because the Arab populations considered the sanctions to be the creation of the United States – maintained only as a means of stealing oil and oppressing the Iraqi people. The lifting of sanctions would alleviate these tensions and thereby reduce the threat of al-Qaida terrorism. On the other hand, a new Iraq would be able to cooperate constructively with the U.S. on the issue of the Israeli-Palestinian conflict, shift some of the oil dependency away from Saudi Arabia, and serve as a new base for American military deployments instead of the difficult Saudi kingdom. Finally, the neoconservatives argued that a liberated and democratic Iraq would serve as an example for the other Arab populations, and would thus set off a domino effect of popular demands of freedom and democracy in the un-free Middle East.[58] The key to a strategic solution in the region, then, according to the neoconservatives, was the military removal of Saddam Hussein.

This construal of the problems in the Middle East gained momentum from the terrorist attacks on September 11, 2001. To be sure, no direct connection existed between 9/11 and Iraq, although several attempts have been made to link the attacks to Iraqi intelligence, but the terrorist events, according to this understanding, originated in the exacerbated tensions in the Middle East, and the key to the solution of these lay in Iraq. On these grounds, people like Wolfowitz argued that attacking Iraq was the most appropriate response to the terrorist attacks of 9/11. Others, led by Colin Powell, managed to convince the President that the response had to be aimed at the Taliban and al-Qaida in Afghanistan – but Iraq was not abandoned, merely postponed.[59]

What Went Wrong?
Motivating assumptions made prior to the war turned out not to be accurate, as no weapons of mass destruction, let alone any evidence that the regime of Saddam Hussein had produced such weapons during the late 1990s and at the beginning of the new millennium, had been discovered.[60] While the connection made between Iraq and al-Qaida may have been very doubtful before the war, according to the American State Department post-war Iraq has become a magnet for al-Qaida warriors. These warriors carry out terrorist acts and kidnappings inside Iraq, while also receiving training which can be put to use in the perpetration of terrorist attacks elsewhere, for instance in the rest of the Middle East and in Europe.[61] The reality facing the American-led coalition in Iraq after

the war thus differed widely from pre-war expectations. Combined with the fact that efforts to secure the widest possible alliance in support for the war had failed, this meant that the post-war difficulties politically turned out to be both different and much greater than expected. While the political process in Iraq, despite the continued violence, has moved forward, and a will to compromise in the period leading up to the December 2006 parliamentary election has been shown, terrorism, sabotage and armed assaults on coalition forces as well as Iraqi forces persistently represent a substantial security problem.[62] Most disconcerting in this respect is the fact that the American forces and intelligence agencies have failed to produce even a rough description of those who are responsible for the terrorist activity and insurgency in Iraq. This leaves the coalition as well as the new Iraqi authorities facing an indistinct enemy, whose organization, strategy and strength is largely unknown.[63]

The lack of concrete knowledge concerning the identity of those responsible for the insurgency and terrorism, combined with the misjudgment of the weapons programs and the obvious absence of understanding

After the American bombings of the Tora Bora Mountains in Afghanistan forced the al-Qaida leaders to flee, the al-Qaida Jihad was gradually taken over by the Jordanian Abu Musab al-Zarqawi, who has carried out numerous terrorist attacks in Iraq.

of Iraqi society which has characterized the course of the American military presence in Iraq, have by themselves given rise to speculations concerning American intentions in Iraq. It has also formed a basis for criticism and mistrust within the United States and in Iraq as well as internationally – especially among opponents of the war in Iraq and particularly in the Middle East. The question is not whether the intelligence has been substandard – that is obviously true – but *why* this has been the case. Presumably, the reasons are threefold: that the United States did not have good sources inside Iraq prior to the war and has not acquired any since then, that those planning the war listened to the wrong people, and that they, through the Pentagon office charged with the vetting of intelligence sources,[64] chose to listen to the sources which would confirm their theory, and to ignore sources from the CIA and the State department which were at variance with or contradicted their theory. What could possibly have motivated this course of action – bad faith, naïveté, cynicism or political priorities – will be a subject for discussion for many years to come and cannot be determined here. The problem for Iraq is that the country is involved in a political conflict the course of which nobody can predict – not even the American government, according to statements made by the President and the Secretary of State in May 2005.[65]

This unfortunate state of affairs has spawned a brand new genre of writings concerning the situation in Iraq which may be termed the 'what went wrong'-genre. Theories and interpretations abound, including a very many different guesses or suggestions as to the causes of the situation. They range from unadulterated conspiracy theories which postulate that the United States never intended to rebuild Iraq, but was all along only looking to rob the country of its resources; through accusations of incompetence and naïveté aimed mainly at the Pentagon and analysts at the White House; to more sober examinations of the complexity of the process. One common denominator of the many contributions, and to some extent of the acknowledgements of at least some of those responsible in Washington, however, is this: that the assessment of the situation in Iraq prior to the war was both overly optimistic and wrongly focused on preventing problems involving masses of refugees rather than on ensuring basic supplies – which either left the interim government with no real plans for the rebuilding of the country, or meant that the existing plans did not take the actual course of events into account. The vision of those, especially at the Pentagon and at the White House, who planned the war was inspired by developments in Eastern Europe after the Cold War, which basically entailed that most of the work would have been taken care of with the overthrow of Saddam Hussein. Once this had been accomplished, the Iraqis, presumably craving freedom, democracy and economic progress, with the assistance of the United States and the international community, would gratefully and swiftly assume responsibility for the development of the new Iraq.[66] This is the theory which has been termed naïve by some and cynical by others, because they consider it mere rhetoric meant to legitimize underlying strategic and military interests. Whether the theory reflects naïveté or cynicism or is simply based on faulty intelligence concerning the situation in Iraq will not be determined here. Suffice it to assert that this was in fact the vision from which the planners of the war were working.[67]

According to this vision the war itself presented the greatest challenge in the liberation of Iraq: for one thing, it had to be quick and efficient, involving as few civilian casualties and as little material damage as possible. It also had to be carried out without creating large numbers of refugees, like those which had resulted from the war in 1991. Furthermore, there should be a clear promise that the situation after Saddam Hussein would in every way be markedly better that it had been under his dictatorship.[68] Actually the war did turn out to be short and, compared to the war in 1991, the casualties were few. In preparation for the war, from the fall of 2002 until the start of the war on March 20, 2003, the United States went to great pains to provide for potentially great numbers of refugees. This was accomplished through secret, yet later publicly confirmed, negotiations with Iran about the securing of the border, and through the establishment of potential refugee camps equipped with tents, food and medicine along the Turkish border.[69] And the promises of a brighter future were repeated over and over. Political analysts have noted that particularly the last two factors contributed to the way in which, from the outset, the efforts at economic reconstruction went wrong.[70] Firstly, the focus on the refugee problem entailed that the safeguarding of Iraqi government institutions was assigned a lower priority, which left them open to looters. Secondly, the American promises of greatly improved conditions were sharply at odds with the actual situation: the contrast between obvious military efficiency and the failure to get simple electrical utilities up and running was disconcerting. Despite satisfaction with being rid of Saddam, experiences like these gave rise to skepticism and mistrust of the U.S.-led military presence in Iraq. This was exacerbated by the violent conduct of the Americans in their hunt for insurgents, and of course by the *Abu Ghraib* affair which brought to light evidence of American torture of Iraqi prisoners.

Iraq – A Collapsed State

Until the beginning of the 1980s, the Iraqi economy was one of the healthiest in the Middle East. Large oil revenues were invested in health, education, infrastructure, and state industries. The war against Iran from 1980 to 1988 caused the economy to stagnate and put the country deep in debt. This was one of the things Saddam Hussein tried to rectify with the occupation of Kuwait in 1990. From an economic perspective, the small but rich emirate with its access to the Gulf and large oil reserves would both fill the gap in the Iraqi Treasury and provide Saddam Hussein with further income and control over the shipping of oil. Instead, the Kuwait venture resulted in a critically destructive war. Besides widespread destruction, more than a hundred thousand deaths, and almost three million refugees,[71] the war also led to Iraq's population being subjected to comprehensive economic sanctions, which completely crippled the country's potential for economic development.[72] Securing Saddam Hussein's power was awarded the highest priority in terms of economic policy, which meant the handing out of privileges to the elite, the leadership of the military and intelligence services, while simultaneously buying the loyalty of Sunni tribal leaders and imams. This brought to a halt the process of development and modernization, and the results were devastating for the Iraqi people as well as for the Iraqi economy.

When the American-led coalition invaded Iraq in March 2003, the country had been transformed into one of the weakest economies of the Middle East, marked by a humanitarian disaster, an absence of production output and development, a run-down and inefficient agricultural sector, a destroyed infrastructure, widespread corruption, and a large black market for smuggled goods run by rival groups of different ethnic affiliations. The Coalition Provisional Authority (CPA) was thus faced with a daunting challenge when, in April 2003, it assumed responsibility for the Iraqi economy. The war did not help matters. Apparently the damage was not nearly as extensive as during the war in 1991, just as the number of refugees and victims was relatively low. But even during, and especially after, the war, the country was in a state of chaos, with rampant theft from the many government institutions which were left unprotected after the fall of the regime. In fact, the Americans only guarded the oil ministry, while other government buildings, public offices, hospitals, schools, factories, power plants and cultural institutions were looted by Iraqis searching for anything of value, or sabotaged by insurgents. The outcome was a marked deterioration in living conditions for the Iraqi people, and huge administrative obstacles for the economic reconstruction.

The Iraqi central government was in ruins, which meant that there were no institutions for the coalition to take over, let alone any reliable statistics, plans or projects in place in the Iraqi ministries for it to refer to – they simply did not exist. Also, the coalition did not have access to any assistance from Iraqis familiar with the country's economy and experienced in the field of public administration, because these had either been killed, jailed or fired, on the grounds that the coalition refused to employ or consult people affiliated with Saddam Hussein's Baath Party. Instead, just short of two thousand Iraqis without any extensive public service experience or insight in terms of development planning, economics and public works were hired to assist the American administration, which was in the main made up by experts deployed by the United States Department of Defense who were less than knowledgeable about conditions in Iraq. The plan was that these two groups were to work together to stabilize the country's economy and initiate the process which would lead to a liberal market economy.[73] The inspiration for this process derived from post-Communist developments in Eastern Europe, where former centralist states within a few years carried out liberalization and privatization in order to adapt their economic policies to the Western capitalist model. But Iraq was not an Eastern European country, it did not have relatively intact governmental institutions which had to be readapted after a velvet revolution, something which in itself has turned out to be a very difficult process; rather, it was a collapsed state with no operational institutions whatsoever.

Under these circumstances, that the coalition actually managed quite swiftly to stabilize the economy is quite impressive and must be considered a success. In a report from *United States Institute of Peace*, Anne Ellen Henderson presents an insightful analysis of developments during the occupation, finding that compared with other post-war situations, the CPA actually achieved good results quite rapidly. Among the successes Henderson counts the fact that the CPA quickly managed to reestablish the distribution of food rations to almost all Iraqi households; to introduce a new monetary standard and stabilize the exchange rate; to implement a liberalization of prices without it leading to rampant inflation; to rebuild the economic governmental ministries; and also to draw up regulations for market oriented banking, taxing, trade and investments; to reestablish a number of schools, health centers and hospitals; to increase rapidly the production of electricity and oil; and to make sure that smaller initiatives intended to fulfill local needs throughout Iraq received support.[74] In other words, considering the bleakness of the initial situation, things could have gone much worse than they actually did.

Henderson's list of absent results and downright failures, though, is even longer. She counts among the shortcomings the fact that the looting of infrastructure and production facilities was not successfully prevented; that sufficient foreign investments were not obtained; that the new economic regulations were not successfully implemented; that the state owned companies were not successfully privatized and put into operation; job creation failed; efforts to improve supplies of electricity considerably relative to the level achieved under Saddam Hussein failed; so, too, did attempts to stabilize oil exports at a level at least similar to that before the war, and also the discontinuation of subsidies on energy, including gasoline, and food; efforts to control corruption were unsuccessful and, significantly, only a fraction of the billions of U.S. dollars allocated by Congress and the World Bank to actual rebuilding projects in Iraq had in fact been put to use.[75]

The lack of security and order continues to present a serious problem for the reconstruction of Iraq. In the immediate aftermath of the war, the lives of Iraqis were made insecure and the rebuilding process obstructed primarily by looting, sabotage, and by 'a guerilla-like war,' a phrase coined by General John Abizaid in July 2003, when he replaced Tommy Franks as Commander of the United States Central Command (CENTCOM). The situation deteriorated in August 2003, when terrorist attacks against the Jordanian Embassy and the newly established headquarters of the UN compelled the latter to withdraw from Iraq. In the south, one of the most important Shia leaders, Ayatollah Muhammad Bakr al-Hakim, along with about eighty others, was killed in a bombing. Foreign companies continued to operate in Iraq up until April 2004, when the violence started to escalate in earnest with a significant rise in the number of attacks on coalition forces, Iraqi politicians and police, and kidnappings of foreigners. From April 2004, only the wealthiest foreign companies remained. This constitutes a key reason why the rebuilding process made slow progress or stopped entirely. Though CPA personnel were able to travel outside of Baghdad in early 2003, for security reasons they soon retired permanently to the heavily guarded Baghdad Green Zone which houses government offices and foreign embassies. Transport outside of the zone preferably took place by helicopter or under heavily armed escort. This helps to explain why the CPA on the one hand was quite successful

After the war in Iraq it was important for George W. Bush to show that the United States is in control of the situation. In 2003 he therefore shared his Thanksgiving turkey with American troops in Baghdad.

in drawing up regulations in support of a transition to a market economy, yet on the other hand had great difficulties implementing these in Iraqi everyday life.[76] The escalation of violence thus resulted in the widespread stalling of the rebuilding process, which meant that the frustration and mistrust among ordinary Iraqis grew, and which also led to an increase in recruiting and support for the insurgents. These problems formed the background for the American decision to expedite the transfer of authority from the CPA to a provisionally appointed Iraqi government, which happened on June 28, 2004.

The Unavoidable Fragmentation of the Dictatorship

The escalation of violent activity in the spring of 2004 and the challenge posed by the holding of parliamentary elections in January 2005 left little room for the new government to concentrate on economic reconstruction and rebuilding. This task was in effect postponed until a new government had been appointed, which did not happen until May 2005. Unfortunately, the formation of the new government did not have the effect of alleviating the violence, and soon insurgency and terrorism once again dominated the agenda in Iraq. While the 2005 elections undoubtedly demonstrate that the Iraqi population is ready for political compromise and accepting of the notion of a peaceful Iraq based on the political process – as illustrated by the fact that, in insisting on voting, many Iraqis bravely defied threats of violence – these very elections have also caused growing divisions within Iraqi society between religious and ethnically based political groups. The distribution of votes reflects the fact that the political agenda is largely decided by clan and tribal affiliations, as well as religious and ethnic loyalties. This tendency of the Iraqi citizen to identify with his or her own group, rather than with the nation as such, has been exacerbated by the manner in which the political process has been staged and orchestrated by the United States. They based their plan for a new Iraq on the assumption that the Iraqi people consisted of three coherent groups: Kurds, Arab Sunni Muslims, and Shia Muslims. The American plan for the transition to a democratic Iraq no doubt contributed to the fragmentation of Iraqi society, but the root cause can be traced back to the days of Saddam Hussein, when the regime increasingly made its exercise of power dependent upon local political forces in the form of tribal leaders and religious authorities.[77]

Yet absolute loyalty to the dictator, rather than ethnicity or religious affiliation, was the primary criterion for becoming a member of Saddam Hussein's regime. Although his personal bodyguard and elite troops were primarily recruited among Sunnis from his own and allied clans, many Shias were to be found among those who zealously and with violent means carried out the task of securing Saddam's power. Hence numerous high ranking Shias could be found in the military and the police, which also employed Kurds. Because of this, the army was more of a national Iraqi army, where loyalty to the Iraqi state was required, than a Sunni Muslim Arab stronghold. Where the regime's efforts to control the Kurdish areas were concerned, Kurds too held positions of trust. Saddam Hussein's power apparatus, then, actually comprised representatives from all parts of Iraqi society; not solely Sunni Muslims, as is sometimes implied. The line along which Iraqi society was divided, into the oppressed and their oppressors, was thus not primarily of an ethnic or religious nature. Rather the division was one between, on the one hand, those who identified with the Iraq of Saddam Hussein, and, on the other, the rest of the population. It was therefore not the case that Iraqi society clearly consisted of three homogenous constituent parts divided into the aforementioned groups; these groups were extensively fragmented internally, and dividing lines often bisected each of the three groups. On the other hand, this does not mean that some measure of identification based on religious and ethnic identity did not exist. This was enhanced during the rule of Saddam Hussein, in part because of his brutal subjection of the Kurds, whom he considered a direct threat to the Baghdad regime, and of the Shia Muslims, whom he feared would ally themselves with the arch enemy, neighboring Iran. Another contributing factor was that he increasingly, especially after the sanctions were imposed, extended his control throughout the regions by relying upon local leaders who, for their part, exercised their power through loyalty to, for instance, the religious group they themselves led: the power base of the dictatorship became fragmented as a result of its own policy of divide and conquer.

The Islamization of Iraqi Society
To achieve some understanding of why violence and the fragmentation of Iraqi society, rather than an eagerness to rebuild Iraq as a nation and a democracy, came to dominate the agenda after the fall of Saddam

Hussein, one must examine the political developments in Iraq during Saddam Hussein's war against Iran as well as the state of affairs after the Gulf War in 1991. At this point Saddam Hussein, due both to the sanctions and the conflict with the international community, and, not least, for reasons of domestic politics, was forced to reconstruct the network on which his power, and that of the Baath Party, was based. The exceedingly harsh policy of subjection, ethnic cleansing and Arabization, which characterized the treatment of the Kurds in the North by the Saddam regime, particularly during the 1980s, has obviously made the Iraqi Kurds extremely wary of and reluctant towards the notion of once again being ruled by an Arab government in Baghdad. They wish to maintain and preferably expand the regional independence they achieved after the Gulf War in 1991. In terms of territory, they are especially concerned with the oil-rich areas around Kirkuk in which they have shown great interest since the war in 2003, despite the fact that they did not lie within the Kurdish autonomous region. Given their shared interest in toppling Saddam Hussein, Kurdish militias fought on the side of the coalition during the American invasion of Iraq. The demand that their independence be maintained – preferably as part of a federalized Iraq, or, if its independence should become subject to threat, in the form of an independent state – together with the sustained interest in Kirkuk, entails a constant risk of bringing the more secular Kurds into conflict with the Shia Muslims as well as with the Arab Sunni Muslims, and also with American interests.

Since the time of the Ottoman Empire, Arab Sunnis have been in power in Baghdad. Constituting a minority of the country's population, Sunnis have had to form shifting alliances to remain in power. After the ascension of Saddam Hussein and the influx of oil revenues, the regime was able to purchase loyalty. This particularly benefited Saddam Hussein's own tribe, but other Sunni Arab tribes, along with the army elite, the Revolutionary Guard, the intelligence services, various foreign and Iraqi businessmen, artists, journalists and, as mentioned before, loyal Shias and Kurds, all benefited as well.[78]

The war against Ayatollah Khomeini's Iran, however, necessitated an adjustment of the national myth, which had previously presented Saddam Hussein as a secular and nationalistic pan-Arabic leader. In order, among other things, to ensure economic and military support from the conservative Sunni Muslim states in the Gulf, which at this point were very worried about the danger of the Iranian Shia revolution spreading to the Shiite minorities on the Arab Peninsula, Saddam Hussein presented himself and Iraq as the defenders of Sunni Islam, pitted against Khomeini's heretical Islamic doctrine. Mosques materialized throughout Iraq, and a kind of grassroots-Islamization accelerated, supported by the regime in Baghdad.[79] Teachers, sheiks and imams from Saudi Arabia, the stronghold of Wahhabism, together with members of the Muslim Brotherhood from Egypt and Palestine, arrived in Iraq, where new Islamic networks, supported by Islamic charities, were established.

When Iraq entered into the ceasefire agreement with Iran in 1988, and subsequently came into head-on confrontation with the Arab states in the Gulf with the occupation of Kuwait in 1990, the myth required further readjustment, this time in order to represent the Arab states in the Gulf as the new arch enemy.[80] Islamic conferences were held in Iraq, and members of the Muslim Brotherhood commuted between seminars in Mecca and Medina and cities in Iraq. This activity was financed by private Saudi foundations sympathetic to Salafism. Local Iraqi leaders in this way allied themselves with the Islamic opposition in Saudi Arabia, which saw the royal family in Riyadh as having fallen from the true path of Islam. Hereby Islamism, inspired by Salafism, was introduced into parts of the Sunni Arab community, and also into small parts of the Kurdish areas. The American-led Western war, and the sanctions which followed it and were backed by the Arab states in the Gulf – and Israel – could, against the backdrop of the Islamic readjustment of the Iraqi national myth, be presented as a clash of civilizations: heretical Arab Muslims of the Gulf region, infidel Christians, and Jews attacked the true Sunni Muslim country, Saddam Hussein's Iraq. This made the defeat in 1991 understandable as well as explicable.[81] The grassroots-Islamization process continued throughout the 1990s, reaching into the heart of the Iraqi government and the core of the Baath Party. From the mid-1990s, formerly secular Saddam heroines, who used to dress in the styles of the West, such as for instance Huda Ammash – who in the period leading up to and during the war in 2003 became known in the West as 'Doctor Germ' – would appear dressed in headscarves.[82] It was however impossible to control the Islamization, and an increasing number of Islamist groups and networks began to oppose the regime. When in 2003 the Americans dissolved the Baath Party, with its attendant networks and strongholds, the new Islamist networks were ready to fill in the remaining gap, and from these many of the insurgents and terrorists are recruited.[83] Those groups which had enjoyed great privileges under Saddam, and which were thus the real losers in terms of the regime change in Baghdad, of course also provided part of the inflow. Finally, it has been noted that the dissolution of the Iraqi army sent up to 350,000 armed soldiers into unemployment, and that the insurgents also receive both recruits and arms from among this large group.

Traditionally, religious Shia Muslims have advocated a quietist attitude towards the regime in Baghdad. This attitude has, on the one hand, facilitated an adjustment to the powers that be, while, on the other hand, creating a distanced attitude to the everyday political process.[84] This tradition has been carried on by the leader of the Shia Muslims, Ali Sistani. The position led to a kind of social agreement between the religious Shiite community, whereby the community was allowed to collect donations, in return for their refraining from any political activism or criticism of the government in Baghdad. This did not mean that the Shiite Imams considered the regime to be legitimate, only that their strategy was to put up with the existing state of affairs in anticipation of better days ahead.

Throughout the 1970s, however, a politicization and an actual reorganization took place in certain circles within the Shiite community, inspired in part by the Communist parties and motivated by a powerful social commitment. The Sadr family in particular was behind the project, but when they began too strongly to oppose the regime, and to be too sympathetic with the Iranian leader Ayatollah Khomeini, their leaders were murdered by Saddam Hussein's security forces. The first victim was Baqir al-Sadr in 1980, followed by Sadiq al-Sadr in 1999.[85] Sadr supporters were mainly recruited from the impoverished Baghdad suburb of Saddam City, which after the war in 2003 was renamed Sadr City. This is also where, with the support of Iran, Sadiq al-Sadr's son, Moktada al-Sadr, has been recruiting for his Mahdi militia, which in 2004 twice challenged Ali Sistani's leadership in Najaf and also confronted the American-led coalition forces.

In 1982, Shia Muslims who had fled to Iran during the Iran-Iraq War formed another political organization, SCIRI (*The Supreme Council of the Islamic Revolution in Iraq*). Their leader was Ayatollah Muhammad Baqir al-Hakim, who managed to establish a militia of several thousand men which returned to Iraq in July 2003. Al-Hakim was killed in a bombing in August of that year. Yet the militia, together with Sistani's organization and al-Sadr's Mahdi militia, continue to be very influential with the Shiite coalition, which won the parliamentary elections in December 2005. The SCIRI in particular, with its armed Badr organization is successfully mobilizing within the Shia community, to the extent that Ali Sistani has been relegated to a less prominent position.[86] Like the Kurds, the Shia community was eager to see Saddam Hussein removed. They were, however, highly skeptical of the Americans, because the United States, after the war in 1991, had failed to support a Shiite rebellion against Saddam Hussein, despite the fact that it had been encouraged by then President George H.W. Bush. Consequently, while they supported the war against Saddam Hussein, they certainly did not support the American occupation. In spite of their animosity towards the Americans, they have managed to exploit the Americans' forced democratization of Iraq, as they, together with the Kurds, have entirely taken over power in Baghdad. Yet internal divisions still run deep within both population groups.

The division of Iraqi society, then, was exacerbated by the political developments under Saddam Hussein, especially during the time of the UN sanctions. The division has been enhanced after the war in 2003, due to the political process which the Americans, in cooperation with the new Iraqi leaders, launched after the toppling of Saddam Hussein. Four groups emerge: Firstly, a large group of dethroned leaders of the Saddam regime and marginalized Baath Party members and discharged army, police, state and municipal employees. Secondly, the Kurds, who achieved self-rule in 1991 and ideologically represent secularization and the notion of a federal Iraq. Thirdly, the Arab Sunnis, some of whom identify with the Salafists, while others are secular nationalists. Fourthly, the Shias, a majority of whom have so far backed Ali Sistani's call for participation in the political process in the interest of ensuring that the new Iraq will be Shia-dominated, and that Islam is affirmed as a significant part of the constitution. Meanwhile, however, the Iranian-supported Shiite SCIRI Party, led by Abd al-Aziz al-Hakim, together with Moktada al-Sadr's group, have gained increasing influence and power at the expense of Sistani's movement. Al-Hakim's objective is to create a strong Shiite state within Iraq, south of Baghdad, and many feel that since the 2005 election Iraq does in fact consist of two states, a Kurdish one in the north and a Shiite one in the South centered in Baghdad. This leaves a barren territory, without any potential for development, for the Sunni Arabs.[87] Sunni motivation for supporting an insurgence grows as the other factions consolidate their positions.

Towards a Civil War in Iraq?

In 2005, as part of the power struggle over a new constitution, the Kurds and the Shias entered into a compromise: the Kurds got their wish for a federally structured Iraq, while the Shias managed to establish that sharia must be an essential factor in the legislative work of the new state. The losers in the political process were the Sunni Arabs, who failed to exert any influence upon the final wording of the new Iraqi constitution due to their boycotting of the January 2005 elections for the assembly to draft the constitution.[88] The constitution was passed by referendum in October 2005. At the parliamentary elections in December 2005, the Shiite *United Iraqi Alliance* was victorious. In the coming years, essential aspects of the constitution must be renegotiated by the new National Assembly. This means that the following issues will be discussed: the future role of the regions in the new Iraq; the distribution of state oil revenues; control of strategically vital oil fields; and the role of Islam in the state of Iraq, including which form or interpretation of Islam will prevail. The Shiite Islamists have the upper hand in this process, but will meet with strong opposition from the Kurds, who refuse to give sharia, Islamic law, the influence it would have if given essential status in a new constitution, and from the Sunni Arabs, many of whom prefer Islamic rule in Iraq, but certainly not in the form of what they see as a heretical Shiite interpretation of Islam. With the December 2005 elections, the process of transition to a new Iraq entered its critical phase, where the struggle between Iraq's numerous groups and factions for power, resources, territory and fundamental values will take place.

Negotiations over decisive issues concerning the formation of a new order in Iraq are officially scheduled to take place in connection with the renegotiation of central aspects of the constitution in the new parlia-

Iraqi elections are not only taking place within the country itself, but anywhere that houses Iraqi refugees from the regime of Saddam Hussein. This photograph shows an Iraqi woman participating in the elections for the Iraqi National Assembly in December 2005.

ment. Yet the Sunni Arabs are voicing their pessimism and frustration at the fact that, as they see it, the premises for the new order have in fact already been settled upon without their participation. As they see it, the Kurds have already established themselves within a state of their own, while the Shia Muslims are assuming a monopoly of power in Baghdad, from which they have launched a systematic purging of Sunni Arabs from all positions of influence within the new power apparatus. In their perspective, the purging of all Baathist elements equals the removal of Arab Sunnis. They point to the fact that operatives from Moktada al-Sadr's Mahdi militia dominate the Ministry of Health and Transportation, from which they blatantly discriminate against Arab Sunni Muslims. This is even more true of the Ministry of the Interior which, since April 2005, was run by Bayan Jaber Solagh, a member of the inner circle of SCIRI. Sunnis accused him of running the secret prisons in which the Americans discovereded the bodies of Sunni Arabs who had been subjected to torture. He was also accused of recruiting death squads from among the members of SCIRI's Badr organization. Introduced into the police force, at night they murder Sunni Arabs, either for the purpose of avenging deeds perpetrated under the Saddam regime, or simply as a cleansing measure. The Minister of the Interior did not deny that, on a daily basis, men dressed as police were in fact responsible for the murder of Sunnis. Without great conviction, he explained that the perpetrators are criminals and murderers who have managed to infiltrate the police force. Whatever the case may be, it is certain that at the top levels of Iraqi politics conflicts persist which are undoubtedly determined by religious affiliations. In a similar manner, the recruiting offices for the army and the police are divided according to religious and ethnic affiliations. This causes concerns that the conflicts and the violence between Sunnis and Shias are not confined to extremist elements, but are much more widespread and rooted in an actual power struggle.[89] The bombing of the Great Mosque in Samarra on February 22, 2006, and the subsequent fighting between Sunnis and Shias, constitute a violent expression of this power struggle, and of the fact that certain forces have an interest in sparking a civil war. Violent attacks aimed at the Shia community had previously been carried out, but each time it had been possible to curb the reaction. Although no Sunni rebel group has assumed responsibility for the attacks, it is generally assumed that Jihadists belonging to this element were behind them. The Jordanian al-Qaida leader Abu Musab al-Zarqawi in particular has been singled out, because he, more or less indirectly, has been known repeatedly to encourage the carrying out of attacks on Shias.[90] Insurgents have become increasingly better organized and have settled upon a strategy which, on the one hand, is aimed at expelling the Americans from the country through the waging of a war of attrition and, on the other, at attacking collaborators and the oil industry, while hostage takings and attacks on Iraqi civilians have been scaled back; meanwhile, they have argued against attacking Shia Muslims with a view to starting a civil war. The strategy has been to drive the United States out of Iraq, not to create chaos.[91] Concurrently, Zarqawi's group has become integrated into the insurgency, instead of continuing to operate on its own, well funded by Jihadists outside of Iraq. The attack on the Great Mosque, then, can be seen as an expression of an escalation of the insurgency, aimed at fighting the American-backed takeover and consolidation of power by the Shias. Leaders such as Moktada al-Sadr and al-Hakim, who are more militant and Shiite nationalist than Ali Sistani, have placed their people in power in Baghdad after the January 2005 elections. As a result Sunni Arabs are increasingly inclined to and justified in viewing them as the immediate enemy, which, in its pursuit of power, has allied itself with the United States – as collaborators.

The risk that Iraq will become fragmented by internal conflicts, with the danger of developing into a civil war proper, is thus imminent, and can presumably only be prevented by means of the continued presence of foreign troops for many years to come. On the other hand, the very presence of foreign troops, American in particular but, after the Muhammad debacle, also Danish troops, in itself constitutes a problem, as illustrated by the continuing insurgency and terrorist activities. Although a growing demand in Congress for a so-called exit strategy forced George W. Bush to present a schedule for the American strategy in Iraq,[92] it seems probable that a stable order will be several years in the making. The regime change in Iraq opened up a Pandora's box of Sunni and Shiite forces which, for years to come, will threaten Iraqi stability and her transition to a liberal and democratic rule, as well as present a frame of reference for anti-Western Islamist elements in, for instance, the Middle East and Europe. The American strategy, based on the domino theory which hypothesizes that the democratization of Iraq will spread in the form of a wave of democracy throughout the Middle East, has so far had quite the opposite effect: a wave of anti-democratic Islamism, which in Iraq and throughout the Middle East has strengthened the opposition to the West and towards the war on terrorism which is waged in the sacred name of democracy and freedom. Denmark is party to this war, and the protests against the Muhammad drawings must be seen in this perspective: the drawings are not the reason why Danish embassies are attacked, but they present an opportunity which is used politically, as a means of inciting a rebellion against the militant battle over values fought by the West in the Middle East and South Asia.

Hamas, Hariri and Iran

Not only problematic developments in Iraq, but also the fact that the Israeli-Palestinian conflict now seems to be irresolvably deadlocked, contribute to this growing atmosphere of mistrust of the West's democratic revolution in the Middle East. The violence between Palestinians and Israel exploded into a longstanding armed conflict after the breakdown of the Camp David negotiations in 2000, which was caused in part by the Israeli refusal to surrender sovereignty over *al-Haram al-Sharif*, the location of the Dome of the Rock as well as the al-Aqsa Mosque – which is even more important to Islamic tradition – on the Temple Mount in East Jerusalem; and also by Yasser Arafat's inability, in his words to Clinton, to exchange the Israeli occupation of the locality in question for actual Israeli sovereignty over it.[93] Repeated attempts at resolving the conflict and resuming negotiations failed, and beginning in the spring of 2002, Israel and the United States refused any negotiations with the leader of the Palestinian Authority, Yasser Arafat, whom they accused of being directly involved in terrorist attacks against Israel.[94]

In the absence of a legitimate Palestinian negotiating partner, the United States and the West pushed for reforms in the Palestinian Authority, which would lead to the creation in 2003 of the office of prime minister. The intention was to push aside Arafat and negotiate with the new leader, Mahmoud Abbas, but it soon became obvious that his authority in Palestine was insufficient. Also, Israel preferred to take unilateral steps in an effort to enhance its own security, rather than negotiating. Apart from a short period during the summer of 2003, actual negotiations never took place, and instead Israel, under the leadership of Ariel Sharon, set off on its unilateral course of action.

The death of Arafat in November 2004 paved the way for the election of a new Palestinian leader in January 2005. Mahmoud Abbas, who had earlier been forced to give up the position of prime minister due to a lack of backing, was elected to the presidency of the Authority. Subsequently, he was beset with the attentions of Israel as well as Western leaders who considered Abbas to be, as it were, moderate and pragmatic – and therefore a reliable negotiating partner. Apart from the niceties, negotiations were not resumed and Sharon, in spite of strongly voiced political opposition within his own political base, undauntedly proceeded with his planned course of action for a unilateral resolution of the conflict. This, quite simply, involved both the withdrawal from Gaza without any negotiations with the Palestinians, and the construction of a so-called security barrier, which would physically separate the West Bank – or parts of the West Bank – from Israel. Sharon argued for his strategy by making clear that the two traditional solutions were unrealistic: a Greater Israel, which had been his original strategy, would make it impossible to define Israel as a Jewish state. The Palestinian population grew at a pace several times that of the Jews, and would therefore within the near future comprise the majority within Israel, making the Jews a minority in their own state. Or – if this situation was to be avoided – deportations of Palestinians from the area would be necessary. This is the predicament often referred to as the demographic dilemma. Because the notion of a forcible deportation of millions of Palestinians to, for instance, Jordan, would be considered an entirely unacceptable strategy by the United States and the international community, by much of the Israeli opposition and, obviously, by Jordan, and would thus be both politically and practically unfeasible, Sharon saw a two-state solution as the only real possibility. This, however, was the solution which both the Camp David negotiations and the Oslo Accords had aimed at, and which Sharon had vehemently opposed. He manifested this opposition by means of a media event on September 28, 2000 – the fifth anniversary of the signing of the Oslo Accords. Sharon took that opportunity, under the scrutiny of the cameras and press corps, to take a walking tour of precisely the *al-Haram al-Sharif*, during which he declared that Jerusalem would forever remain an undivided Israeli city. The so-called al-Aqsa Intifada began the very next day. Sharon's stroll was certainly not the reason for the uprising, but rather constituted the event which unleashed many years worth of pent up Palestinian anger and frustration – a development similar to when *Jyllands-Posten*'s drawings of the Prophet triggered an Islamist uprising in the Middle East and Asia. Sharon's problem was that while a Palestinian state seemed to present the only realistic solution to the demographic dilemma, he was willing to give up neither the entire West Bank nor any part of Jerusalem. In both cases, the withdrawal to the territory of the pre-1967 borders would entail the dismantlement of a considerable number of Jewish settlements, as well as a partition of the Holy City. Both were decidedly unthinkable prospects for the Israeli leader.

These were, however, exactly the two core issues of the negotiations between Israel and the Palestinians, as a result of the pressure brought to bear on them by Clinton. Consequently, Sharon's strategy was to avoid negotiations and instead leave Israel to decide on a solution to the territorial issues, including the problem of Jerusalem. The withdrawal from Gaza was accomplished over the summer of 2005, and the construction of the security barrier is to be completed in 2007. The barrier, a massive construction project, is meant to prevent Palestinian suicide bombers from entering Israel as well as to form the border between Israel and a future Palestinian state. It can be seen as a concretization of Israel's definition of the borders of a Palestinian state. If Jerusalem is left out of the picture for the purposes of delimiting the West Bank, as it was by Sharon and still is by his successor Ehud Olmert, the completion of the fence will mean that Israel has annexed 5-7 percent of the West Bank, while the rest is turned over to the Palestinians. If Jerusalem is included in the definition of the West Bank, as the Palestinians of course insist it must be, the part to be annexed by the Israelis is considerably larger, and the Palestinians would furthermore be forced to surrender East Jerusalem. In any case, the territory which Israel intends to turn over to the Palestinians is limited to Gaza, and 90-95 percent of the West Bank excluding Jerusalem, over which Israel insists on maintaining undivided sovereignty.

The United States and the other members of the so-called Quartet[95] never questioned the Israeli argument about the aforementioned lack of a legitimate negotiating partner, and Sharon used it to justify his going ahead with his plan for a unilateral solution; the withdrawal from Gaza even made him look like a genuine peacemaker. Meanwhile the Quartet was pushing for elections to be held in Palestine, which were expected to provide the much missed legitimate negotiating partner. After the elections the negotiations were to be resumed. A part of the insistent American and Western pressure was the requirement that Hamas take part in the election, in spite of the awareness that the party did not accept the premises for the negotiations determined by the Israelis and the Americans, and that Hamas was a militant organization which bore the main part of the responsibility for the numerous suicide attacks against Israeli targets. This was the reason for the inclusion of Hamas on both the EU's and the Americans' list of terrorist organizations. The reason for the requirement that Hamas take part in the elections was that without the representation of this party, the elections could not be considered free and democratic. As early as 2003, in a remarkable article in *Foreign Affairs*, Clinton's top advisor on Middle Eastern policy, Martin Indyk, predicted that the unilateral Israeli strategy would lead to Palestine being dominated by Hamas.[96] This was a view shared by many others, and it should therefore not have surprised the United States and the EU that Hamas might emerge victorious after Palestinian parliamentary elections. This of course was exactly what happened at the Palestinian elections in January 2006, and in February 2006, Hamas leader Ismail Haniya assumed the position of Prime Minister of the Palestinian Authority.

Soon after the Hamas electoral victory, the United States and Israel announced that they refused to cooperate with the new government, and that they intended to halt transfers of funds to the Palestinian Authority. Efforts on the part of Condoleezza Rice to make Arab governments do the same have met with little success. Instead, Rice has been working for a strengthening of the power of the office of President Mahmoud Abbas, efforts to which the Middle East have reacted with a measure of ironic skepticism: during Arafat's chairmanship, the United States and the Quartet, in the name of democracy, pushed for the strengthening of a Palestinian government led by a prime minister. After free elections had been held, and the desired democratic legitimacy of the prime ministerial office had been achieved, they then turn around and, again in the name of democracy, push for the strengthening of the precidency.

The fact that the Palestinians elected Hamas may be due to a desire for an Islamic state, in which sharia constitutes the basis for legislation. Most observers, however, believe the more likely explanation to be that the election result is an expression of protest. Throughout the decade that has passed since Arafat's Fatah Party won the election for the Palestinian Legislative Council, conditions have steadily deteriorated for the Palestinians. In spite of concessions made to Israel by the Fatah leadership with a view to opening negotiations, which would result in the creation of a Palestinian state, this goal actually remains as elusive as ever. The concessions comprise the recognition of the state of Israel; a promise to desist from terrorism and militant activity aimed at Israel; the changing of the statutes of the PLO; the consent to cooperate with Israel and the CIA on matters of security; the acceptance of potential consecutive renegotiations of Oslo 2; as well as the agreement to participate in the Camp David negotiations, in spite of misgivings and the fear that a breakdown of the negotiations would be blamed on them. This enumeration is not an attempt to lay the blame for the failure of the negotiations wholly on Israel. But that is how the matter is commonly viewed by the Palestinians. Hamas actually refrained almost entirely from carrying out terrorist attacks in the period between the exceedingly bloody attacks in the spring of 1996 and the outbreak of the al-Aqsa Intifada. The majority of Palestinians feel that Fatah has made concession upon concession without furthering the cause of an autonomous Palestinian state – if anything, quite the reverse has been achieved. Throughout this period, Hamas has criticized the negotiating strategy of the Fatah leadership, and most Palestinians feel that this criticism has turned out to be justified. In addition, Fatah has been accused of governing the Palestinian Territories with a view solely to securing benefits and privileges for themselves, and to remaining in power. Corruption, nepotism, abuse of power, and the absence of due legal process have, together with the absence of improvements in the living conditions of the Palestinian population, been the order of the day under the Fatah leadership, a state of affairs which Hamas has incessantly, and rightly, pointed out. Of the many billions of dollars which the international community have poured into the Palestinian Authority since the inception of the Oslo Accords, a mere fraction has been used for actual improvements of living conditions. The remainder has been used for more or less private purposes, such as villas in Amman, or has ended up in Arafat's foreign bank accounts, benefiting for instance his widow, Suhair. During the last three years of Arafat's life, she chose a life of luxury in Paris over the difficulties of everyday life in Palestine. If given the choice in connection with a free election, would anyone of sound mind vote for leaders such as these? No. They would vote for the people who all along have been pointing out these discrepancies. And, since in Palestine – as in the rest of the Arab Middle East – no organized liberal and secular opposition exists, because its members have either been killed, jailed, scared silent or have fled to the West, the Islamists in the form of Hamas represented the only alternative.

Idealist visions of the democratization of the Middle East, combined with *realpolitical* preferences for allowing Israel to define the conditions for Israeli-Palestinian negotiations, led to yet another Islamist election victory; in this case, it has caused a setback in the negotiations, to a situation similar to that which persisted before Arafat's 1988 official recognition of the state of Israel, and his declaration that terrorism was to be considered an illegitimate means in the Palestinian struggle for autonomy. Alternatively, the international donors could have demanded that the Fatah leadership use the abundant funds they were given in accordance with their intended purposes: the furthering of good governance, the liberalization of Palestinian society, and the creation of potential for economic growth. This might have lent that legitimacy to the Fatah leaders which would have convinced the Palestinian voters to choose them over the Islamist alternative. Instead, the Palestinians chose Hamas. This forces the West to, yet again, *refuse* to accept the results of a free and fair election, in this case an election which had been staged and enforced by the West itself. Hamas has declared its willingness to observe a ceasefire on the condition that Israel withdraws to the pre-1967 borders. This is unlikely to happen, which is why Hamas refuses to recognize Israel and to disarm. Consequently, the United States and the EU find themselves unable to support the new Palestinian government and forced by pass the government in the provision of humanitarian aid.

The question remains whether free and fair elections are even possible in un-free societies? The result for the Palestinians of their latest election may well be an even worse economic situation than under Fatah, because the United States and the EU are reducing financial support. Meanwhile Israel, after their parliamentary elections in March 2006, can claim that, in the absence of a legitimate negotiating partner, a unilateral Israeli solution constitutes the only viable plan, and proceed to carry it out. The United States and the EU will be hard pressed to find justification for any criticism of the Israeli reasoning and course of action, since both officially consider the new Palestinian leadership to be a terrorist organization.[97] In this way, Israel may manage to distance itself from the Palestinian conflict, which will then become a matter for the international community to deal with. Surely this was not meant to happen – or was it? This question is presently occupying the minds of many in the Middle East. Whatever the case may be, the course of the process of democratization in Palestine provides many Muslims with an occasion for raising questions concerning the intentions of the United States and the West as far as the war against terrorism is concerned, if it is to be considered a project for the promotion of freedom.

In Iraq as well as in Palestine, the West and the United States have forced through regime changes, and, in both places, it is the Islamists who have so far been strengthened in the ongoing battle over values. This has forced the West to compromise on certain political issues where idealistic vision and the necessities of practical politics intersect. From the point of view of the Middle Eastern populations, these compromises contribute to an impression of a hypocritical policy, and thereby to a de-legitimization of the Western project of establishing a democratic order in the Middle East. With Syria and Iran, the United States has adopted a different strategy from that of forced regime change: one of harsh sanctions and political pressure by way of the UN system, which are both underscored by the threat of American military action. With a view to a discussion of the constructive merits of this particular contribution to the battle over values, a brief examination of the American and Western policies in relation to Iran and Syria will be useful.

Syria and Iran
Soon after the end of the war in Iraq in May 2003, the United States stepped up its aggressive rhetoric towards Syria, which was later followed by sanctions passed by Congress in 2004.[98] There was therefore some speculation in the media that Syria might be the next target, after Iraq, of U.S. regime changing efforts by means of military force. Things never went that far, but considerable pressure was put on Syria. The reasons were that the country produced chemical weapons; allowed Palestinian groups such as Hamas and Islamic Jihad to maintain representations in Damascus; actively assisted incoming Jihadists in using Syria as a country of transit into Iraq, where they would join insurgent groups; and that

Syria continued to have troops deployed in its neighboring country, Lebanon, whose foreign policy was entirely controlled from Damascus. Syria's increasingly obvious hold over Lebanese politics culminated in 2004 when Lebanon was pressured into changing its constitution, in order for Emile Lahoud, the presidential candidate favored by the Syrians, to remain in office. This provoked the Lebanese opposition beyond restraint, and demonstrators took to the streets in an effort to expel the Syrians from the country. France was an ally of the Lebanese opposition, and this paved the way for the September 2004 United Nations Security Council Resolution 1559, which was backed by the United States and France; the resolution demanded the withdrawal of Syrian troops, and that Lebanese democracy be respected.[99]

Syria had a number of reasons for wishing to maintain its military presence in Lebanon. First of all, the weak Syrian economy was able to draw much-needed sustenance from Lebanon, Syrian workers could find employment there, and goods which were unavailable in Damascus could be brought in from Beirut. The members of the Syrian government and security apparatus in particular gained from the presence in Lebanon, as it increasingly benefited their private interests rather than the Syrian state. Syrian strategic interests were involved, too; among other things, she used her military presence in Lebanon to pressure Israel into giving up their occupation of the Syrian Golan Heights. In negotiating with Israel, Syria brought to bear the fact that they controlled the frequency of Hezbollah attacks across the border into Israel, which meant that any peace with the Hezbollah must be negotiated through Damascus: if Israel would give up the Golan, the Syrians in turn would put a stop to the aggression aimed at Israel on the part of the militia, which received support from Lebanon and Iran. Israeli Prime Minister Ehud Barak stripped the Syrians of this negotiating advantage in May 2000, by simply pulling out of southern Lebanon. Shortly thereafter, Hafiz al-Assad, the powerful president of Syria, died, and was succeeded by his son Bashar, who was much less experienced in the ways of cynical power politics. Consequently, after only a few months, the government in Damascus had become considerably weakened, as its negotiating advantage over Israel was gone and the powerful and experienced president gone. His son, Bashar, is still considered a weak president, pressured by his more experienced and cynical leading politicians and heads of national security. The Syrian insistence on maintaining their presence in Lebanon, even after the Israelis had withdrawn theirs, had a number of causes: economic interests, and the fact that Syria, which is allied with Iran, would remain in a position to guard her strategic interests by serving as a liaison between Iran and Hezbollah, and through this, together with Iran, maintain the pressure on Israel by ensuring the presence of forces allied with the Iranian Islamic Republic at the Israeli front line. In addition, Syria is not on good or close terms with either Egypt, Turkey or the Arab states in the Gulf, which makes a strategic alliance with Iran crucial for the country's ability to avoid complete isolation within the Middle East.

From 2003, Syria came under considerable and increasing external pressure, which was exacerbated by the 2004 UN resolution demanding the withdrawal from Lebanon, and the newly introduced American sanctions, also implemented in 2004. The pressure grew almost explosively with the February 14, 2005 murder of the long-serving Lebanese Prime Minister, Rafik Hariri, in a Beirut car bombing. Hariri had become opposed to the presidency due to his disagreement with the amendment to the constitution which prolonged Lahoud's term. The Lebanese opposition was convinced that Syria was behind the murder, which led to large demonstrations in Beirut, the so-called Cedar Revolution. The demand for Syria to exit Lebanon became increasingly manifest, in spite of equally sizeable demonstrations in support of Syria arranged by the Hezbollah. The outcome was that Syria actually withdrew its troops from Lebanon, and the establishing of a UN commission of inquiry, led by the German lawyer Detlev Mehlis. Their preliminary report was issued in October 2005, and, in spite of the protestations of the Syrians, all indications regarding the Hariri assassination led in the direction of the Syrian leadership.[100]

Although the Syrian Islamists affiliated with the Muslim Brotherhood are forcefully subdued within Syria, where the organization is outlawed and takes its directions from London, they are widely supported by the population They are increasingly dissatisfied with what, to put it gently, can be termed the government's violent means of oppression and the lack of improvements in general living conditions and prosperity. The so-called Damascus Declaration constituted a clear indication of the dawning optimism of the opposition: a loose network of various opposition groups, together with the Muslim Brotherhood, declared that the government lacked the endorsement of the people, and that they welcomed the growing international pressure on the country's leadership.[101] Although the opposition is weak and poorly organized, due to the oppression by the Syrian state and the exile of the organizational branch of the Muslim Brotherhood, it is remarkable that secular groups joined forces with the Islamists in criticizing the Syrian government in the aftermath of the Mehlis report. The report contains concrete accusations against Syria, yet it is cast in doubt because, to some, it remains unclear what Syria stood to gain from the death of Hariri. Apart from the obligatory conspiracy theories – postulating the involvement of Israel or the United States, or even the UN, in the murder of Hariri, their objective being an increase in the pressure on Damascus – the most widely held theory is that leading Syrian politicians with significant personal economic interests were responsible for the assassination. The implication is that wear and tear, corruption and intrigue within the Syrian government has created a situation where Bashar is powerless to control it or keep it coherent. The appearance, certainly, is that of a very weak government.

The Syrian government has thus come under increasing pressure from almost all sides throughout 2004 and 2005: from the UN, the United States and the EU; from its own opposition, weak though it may be; and, finally, from an increasing number of Syrians who support the Islamists. From this perspective, the outcry against *Jyllands Posten*'s Muhammad drawings could be used to vent some of the pent up anger, directing it at Denmark and away from the Syrian government itself. This interpretation is borne out by the fact that the Syrian authorities and security forces remained quite passive on the occasion of the demonstrations which led to the burning of the building which houses the Danish Embassy, on February 4, 2006. The next day, the Danish representation in Beirut was also attacked during tumultuous demonstrations, but a more unclear picture emerges of this episode, although some claim that here, too, there are indications of a Syrian influence.

If the Syrian government consciously intended to use the Muhammad drawings as a vent for relieving the pressure on itself, the effect of this effort was short-lived, as the United States went ahead and intensified its criticism of Syria for having incited an anti-Danish and anti-Western atmosphere. The pressure on Damascus will therefore both continue and increase, and should the final UN report conclude that Syria was in fact responsible for Hariri's assassination, the Security Council will likely implement sanctions against the country. It is hard to predict whether the Syrian government can withstand such pressure – many believe it cannot – and it is even more difficult to predict what may replace it: it is possible that the Islamists will seize power, as they enjoy widespread popular support. The Syrian Islamists, however, are poorly organized, and have no immediate access to the power apparatus, which might entail the risk of internal conflict or perhaps even civil war. Washington relies on the judgment of exiled opposition politicians who believe that liberal and secular forces may be in place to take over power in the event of a breakdown of the regime of Bashar al-Assad. The American strategy regarding Syria, however, differs profoundly from the military regime-change strategy employed in Iraq: in Syria, the Americans are maintaining an increasing pressure on the government in Damascus, assuming, presumably correctly, that in the long run the government will be unable to withstand it.

The United States Takes its Stand on the Muhammad Case
When the United States finally spoke up for Denmark on the Muhammad issue, they launched a rhetorical attack on Syria and Iran, whom they considered to be the main driving forces behind the escalating protests against the drawings, rather than a vehement defense of liberal rights, of which freedom of expression and the right to freely criticize religion are vital to the democratic project. Considering that it was actually Saudi Arabia which caused the escalation of the crisis by recalling its ambassador from Denmark and initiating the trade boycott, and the fact that Egypt played an active and decisive role in creating the controversy in the first place, this seems a rather curious reaction on the part of the Americans. Both Saudi Arabia and Egypt are, however, partners in the American *public diplomacy* project in the Middle East. Also, Saudi Arabia is a necessary and most cooperative partner in the effort to avoid additional increases in already very high oil prices, while Egypt is an important ally in the effort to avoid a further escalation of the Palestinian conflict. The struggle of a small country to defend free speech was too insignificant a cause for the superpower to risk challenging these two countries, as this might have endangered its overall strategic

interests. On the other hand, the United States could not stand idly by while the representations of one of its warfaring coalition partners were assaulted and burned. That the attacks on Danish embassies took place in Damascus, and subsequently in Iran, and that the governments of both countries appeared to be directly involved in the destruction, was a fact which afforded the United States a perfect opportunity to put on record its support for Denmark and assert itself as a defender of free speech, as well as to avoid any significant confrontation with Egypt or the Saudis by aiming its rhetorical outrage at the two countries which were already subject to American sanctions.

Islamic Nationalism on the Rise in Iran
Since 1993, Iran has been subjected to sanctions by the United States, on the basis of allegations that the country supports international terrorism and persists in its illegal production of weapons of mass destruction. Although there have been occasional signs of improvement in the relationship between the United States and the Iranians since the Islamic revolution which led to the formation of the Islamic Republic of Iran, diplomatic connections have been cut off since the Iranian occupation of the American embassy, which took place during the period from November 1979 to the day of Ronald Reagan's inauguration as President in January 1981. Ronald Reagan's 1986 attempt at repairing relations with Iran resulted in the so-called Iran-Contra scandal.[102] After the election of the apparently reform-friendly President Khatami in 1997, a tentative dialogue between the United States and Iran took place, and in connection with the United States' war in Afghanistan in 2001 the Iranians proved their willingness to cooperate, as long it took place within a multilateral framework.[103] And, as mentioned earlier on, the United States and Iran were in touch during the effort to prevent a refugee crisis in connection with the war in Iraq in 2003.

Still, since the revolution the relationship has generally been characterized by conflict and confrontation. The United States toughened its sanctions on Iran in 1995 and 1996, extended them in 2001, and in a 2002 speech to Congress George W. Bush included Iran in the so-called 'axis of evil'. While Iran sees the U.S. Middle Eastern policy as purely an imperialist project, the United States cites three primary reasons for its confrontational strategy: Firstly, Iran supports Hezbollah and the

Palestinian groups Hamas and Islamic Jihad, and is therefore directly involved in terrorists attacks on Israel; secondly, Iran interferes in Iraqi politics; and thirdly, Iran is engaged in the development of weapons of mass destruction.

In 2003 Iran admitted to producing enriched uranium in connection with its nuclear energy program, and to having concealed this activity from international inspectors for years. During Bush's visit to Europe in February 2005, the United States agreed to let the EU head negotiations concerning this issue, while at the same time making it clear that if the efforts of the EU failed to lead to a diplomatic solution, the issue would be brought before the UN Security Council. In 2004 and 2005 American politicians seriously contemplated the possibility of a military solution, while the EU, represented by the United Kingdom, France and Germany, tried to reach an agreement, according to which Iran would accept enriched uranium to be delivered from abroad, rather than continue producing their own.[104] Also, Iran was to allow extensive UN inspection of its nuclear energy program, in return for favorable trade agreements with the EU. Meanwhile, the EU was working on getting China and Russia to back a negotiated solution. But the negotiations foundered and no agreement was reached, and in January 2006, all five permanent members of the UN Security Council decided that Iran was to be brought before the Council under threat of UN sanctions. At first the Iranians, in an almost ritualistic manner, reacted by rejecting the threats, defiantly declaring that they would persist in going forward with their program. It also seemed in accordance with a familiar pattern when, in February 2006, they struck a more cordial tone, and welcomed dialogue and renewed negotiations. Yet, in another characteristic move, they simultaneously resumed their own production of enriched uranium, and rejected a proposal to have the uranium produced in Russia, under strict UN supervision. All parties are interested in a negotiated solution of some kind; deterred by prior experience with UN sanctions in Iraq, nobody really wants sanctions to be the end result, and, also on the basis of developments in Iraq, a military solution seems equally unattractive. The Iranians of course appreciate this dilemma, and carry on a game of cat and mouse by oscillating between, at times, proudly and vehemently rejecting the demands of the international community, and, at others, making conciliatory requests for dialogue and negotiations.

There are three reasons for Iran's refusal to give up their ability to produce their own enriched uranium. The first is a matter of domestic politics: despite widespread hostility towards the Iranian theocracy, a majority of the population, motivated by nationalistic sentiment, supports the government's defense of Iran's right to develop its own nuclear energy program and, for that matter, its own nuclear weapons as well. On this issue, then, there is no agreement between the Iranian opposition's demands for reforms and the American criticism of the nuclear energy program, including the demand that Iran discontinue its production of enriched uranium. In fact, the pressure placed by the international community on the Iranian government regarding this issue seems to strengthen it in the eyes of its population, including those of the opposition. Secondly, Iran sees itself as an ideological force to be reckoned with in the confrontation between Islamism and Western order, and for this reason alone refuses to yield to Western demands for monitoring which are made, not only with reference to international laws and conventions, but are also significantly motivated by the fact that Iran is an Islamic state. These two circumstances are both clear expressions of the battle over values, within the region as well as between the Islamists and the West. The third factor to be taken into account is that Iran, in terms of national security, would indeed gain an enormous advantage from the actual production of a nuclear bomb: three neighboring states, Pakistan, India and Israel, possess nuclear weapons, in addition to which Iran, after the American wars in Afghanistan and Iraq, is now surrounded by American troops. Finally, Iran's relationships with the Arab states in the Gulf are less than friendly. In this sense, the uncertainty surrounding the question of whether the country actually develops nuclear weapons is useful to Iran in relation to regional as well as global security politics. Were Iran to succeed in gaining possession of nuclear weapons, it would strengthen considerably the role of the Islamic Republic as a regional great power. Iran's nuclear policy, then, is based on real national security considerations as well as ideological ones, considerations which are at present inextricably interlaced, and which make it exceedingly difficult for the EU as well as the UN to negotiate a viable agreement with Iran. Israel constitutes an additional, unpredictable factor in the Iranian negotiational double-dealing. There is a risk that Israel may decide to launch a unilateral military attack on Iran, similar to the 1981 bombing of Saddam Hussein's nuclear reactor in Baghdad. As the UN-led negotiations over Iran's nuclear program become further deadlocked, the risk of Israeli or American military intervention grows.

Even before the Muhammad drawings, Iranian President Mahmoud Ahmedinejad had challenged Western notions of free speech, by claiming that the Holocaust had never taken place, and that the Holocaust was merely an invention, a lie, on the part of the West, meant to legitimize the continued existence of Israel. It therefore seemed likely that Iran would react radically to the Muhammad drawings, as in the case of Ayatollah Khomeini's 1989 fatwa against Salman Rushdie. From this perspective, Iran's reaction was relatively calm. This is in no way meant as a defense of the unacceptable Iranian attacks on the Danish embassy, which were facilitated by the authorities: in February 2006, a small group numbering a few hundred individuals were made to demonstrate outside the Danish embassy in Tehran, where Iranian police politely stepped aside to allow the demonstrators to hurl incendiaries at the embassy – after which demonstrators and police allegedly went off to have tea together. However, keeping in mind the Rushdie affair, the occupation of the American Embassy, and the confrontational and provocative rhetoric of the president, the Iranian reaction could have been much worse.[105] Also, the Iranian reaction was curiously delayed; it only occurred after protests had spread from Syria and Lebanon to the Shia-dominated areas of Southern Iraq. Compared with developments in Syria, Lebanon, Pakistan and Indonesia, the reaction in Tehran was moderate. It would be natural to interpret this relative Iranian moderation in the light of Iran's concurrent attempts at avoiding being brought before the UN Security Council on the issue of their production of enriched uranium.

Since the EU gave up hopes of reaching a negotiated solution with Iran, the United States has hardened its confrontational stance against the Islamic republic. At a Congressional hearing Condoleezza Rice described Iran as the most serious threat against American interests, and termed the country a "central banker for terrorism."[106] On March 14, President George W. Bush continued in this vein by accusing Iran of providing insurgents in Iraq with weapons and ammunition.[107] These statements were made while Congress was considering a law which would allocate 75 million dollars to the support of Iranian opposition groups, and for the production of radio and television broadcasts in Persian. These are to be broadcast to the Iranian population, with a view to undermining the government and promoting democracy, a strategy similar to that of the *Iraq Liberation Act* passed in 1997. As was the case with the strategy for Iraq, Eastern Europe served as the role model, as the funds for the promotion of democracy in Iran are given with explicit reference to the American support for the Polish *Solidarnosc* movement, which in the 1980s challenged the governing Communist parties of Poland and the Soviet Union.[108]

As negotiations and critical dialogue with the Iranian government seem unable to lead to an agreement over the Iranian nuclear energy program, two potential strategies emerge with increasing clarity: either a classic containment strategy, which would isolate Iran internationally and subject it to harsh UN sanctions, or a military intervention by Israel or the United States. A containment strategy requires full participation by China and Russia, but both these countries have considerable interests in Iran: Russia's interests are primarily related to business and trade, whereas China relies on Iranian oil and natural gas for a portion of its energy supply. Consequently, it is unlikely that agreement can be reached within the UN Security Council, which leaves the option of military intervention. This would likely not take the shape of an actual regime-change effort, but rather consist of the bombing of Iranian nuclear energy facilities with a view to setting back the Iranian nuclear program by several years. The American rhetoric and the preparations being made in Washington make for a confrontation eerily reminiscent of that leading up to the war in Iraq. And, as Iran is unlikely to stand down, the risk of a military attack taking place in the near future grows considerably. Such an attack would fan the flames of the battle over values, further strengthening the position of the Islamists.[109] In attacking Iran, the United States would be hoping to weaken the government to the extent that the Iranian opposition could accomplish a velvet revolution and, supported by the Americans, begin a process of reform and democratization. This provides a background for appreciating the grant of 75 million dollars mentioned above. Although there is an outspoken desire among young Iranians for reforms, nationalistic sentiment runs deep in Iran. This means that, if faced with a choice between Iranian nationalism, based on Islam, and American-sponsored regime change, there is a risk that they will chose Islamic nationalism over Western democratic values.

The United States is thus sticking to its morally based national security policy as outlined in the beginning of this section. Regime change remains at the top of the security policy agenda, with Syria and Iran next in line after Iraq. For the time being, the means employed are *public diplomacy* and sanctions, in an effort to put determined pressure on the two countries in order to bring about the breakdown of the totalitarian regimes, making room for a popular uprising which, as in Eastern Europe, is supposed to lead to democracy. In both places, however, there is a considerable risk that it will in fact be the Islamists who come out strengthened. Syrian as well as Iranian citizens are highly critical of their governments, and presumably majorities among both populations wish for their governments to be replaced. It would therefore seem natural for them to welcome the American and Western pressure on these governments: the Western objective of preventing Iran from having nuclear weapons should presumably concur with Iranian desire for reforms and democracy. But the pressure applied by the West in fact seems to meet with great resistance, and lead to support for the Islamists. This is likely due to the fact that the underlying moral legitimization for this pressure consists in its presumed ability to bring about Western security through the dissemination of Western values in an ambiguous mixture of idealistic vision and the necessities of *realpolitik* rather than being motivated by a genuine appreciation of demands for rights and security on the part of Muslim and Middle Eastern populations. Neither do the sanctions and *public diplomacy* efforts which have succeeded the *shock and awe*-strategy seem to have led to greater security, or to have facilitated the adoption of Western values. In part 2, I examine the philosophical assumptions underlying the American strategy as seen in the light of the tradition of American security policy; address the question of why the Middle East is the world's least democratic region; and consider some concrete examples of Middle Eastern strategies for adapting to the demands of globalization, which are becoming equally urgent here.

Part 2

The Democratic Dilemma in the Authoritarian Middle East

"Wherever the standard of Freedom and Independence has been or shall be unfurled, there will be heart, her (The United States') heart, her benedictions and her prayers be. But she goes not abroad, in search of monsters to destroy. She is well-wisher to the freedom and independence of all. She is the champion and vindicator only of her own. She commends the general cause by the countenance of her voice, and the benign sympathy of her example. She well knows that by once enlisting under other banners than her own, were they even banners of foreign independence, she would involve herself beyond the power of extrication, in all wars of interest and intrigue, of individual avarice, envy, and ambition, which assume the colors and usurp the standard of freedom. The fundamental maxims of her policy would insensibly change from liberty to force… She might become the dictatress of the world. She would be no longer the ruler of her own spirit."

John Quincy Adams, 1821

Limits to Freedom?

The vision behind the United States' war in Iraq was based on the notion that national security is contingent upon democracy.[110] This is an old notion, proposed by the German philosopher Emmanuel Kant in his book *Perpetual Peace*. Here Kant argued that democratic republics do not make war on one another.[111] But he also emphasized that democracies would feel a strong urge to make war – often brutal and irregular in nature – on non-democracies. An international community of like-minded, democratic states handles conflicts through agreements, negotiations, treaties and, occasionally, through political and economic sanctions, based on international law – because the states which make up such a community are based on a shared set of values, which can be summed up in the concept of liberty. This mode of conflict management is not – at least not always – possible in dealing with non-democratic states, because they do not share these basic values. The project initiated by the United States after the terrorist attacks on September 11, 2001, then, basically constitutes a global battle over values – or, as it were, over cultures – where all available means, including political, economic, diplomatic and military ones, are employed in an effort to propagate democratic values, with a view primarily to ensuring American national security.

Manifest Destiny

This is the project which may be called the globalization of the American order. The vision of a clear interdependency between liberty and security was dominant even during the American Revolution and when the American Union was established in the 19th century. At that time, however, the vision was geographically delimited to what the 1823 Monroe Doctrine defined as the Western hemisphere, meaning the American continent.[112] Ever since American independence was achieved, American politicians have debated the proper geographical limits to the vision. From the mid-19th century, it became increasingly evident that it should be applied from coast to coast, as expressed in the ideology of *Manifest Destiny*, and from Canada in the North to Mexico in the South.[113] Much more controversy surrounded South and Central America, where the new Union early on supported the rebellious states in their struggle to free themselves from their European colonial masters.[114] While it has always been uncertain to which extent the United States should actively support the democratization of this region, through for instance military intervention in the form of preventive strikes, it has always been clear that this was an American area of interest of which the Europeans must stay clear. As such, the Monroe Doctrine is as valid for this area today as it was in 1823. The other aspect of the Doctrine – that the United States would refrain from interfering in conflicts outside of the Western hemisphere – was definitively discarded with Woodrow Wilson's declaration of war against Germany in 1917, which entered the United States into the First World War. The notion that security and democracy are mutually dependent was again established in Wilson's famous wording in the declaration of war: that America was stepping into the war in Europe in order to make *the world safe for democracy*. This formulation was welcomed by Congress – though not by all members – because it resonated with the historical process which had established and so far ensured American freedom through the union of free states. It was met with resistance by some, mainly due to concerns that the implementation of the vision beyond the North American continent would in fact risk undermining the American Union and, with that, the time-honored freedom. These concerns were exacerbated by the failed American ventures in Latin America and the Philippines.[115]

Those who agree with Wilson's notion that American security can only be ensured through the globalization of the American order – which in principle means that the world must become a community of democratic states – and wish to make this project the main priority of American security policy, may be called *revolutionary globalists*.

Those who, on the contrary, agree with Monroe that the security of the Union is best preserved if the vision of the perpetuation and active implementation of the American order is limited to the American continent, may be called *realist regionalists*. Both groups of course share the vision of the mutual dependency of security and democracy. But they differ in the sense that whereas the revolutionaries wish to globalize the vision through an activist policy which is supposed to lead to a string of revolutions in non-democratic states, the realists point out that such a strategy of forced regime change will produce an equal number of enemies of the American order, thereby actually impairing the security of the United States. The revolutionaries envision the utopia of the world community of free states, and are able to refer to the fact that the success of the United States was achieved exactly through 19th century militant expansion, which made the North American continent safe for democracy and freedom. The realists, on the other hand, fear a global civil war, and refer to the fact that it took a civil war over the issue of slavery and the genocide of Native Americans for the American brand of freedom to be extended, not only to white Anglo-Saxon Protestants, but also to blacks and Native Americans, the latter, however, confined to designated reservations by the American order.[116] They also refer to the fact that the United States neither during nor after the First World War faced any strategic threat, and that, accordingly – in the spirit of the Monroe doctrine – there was no reason for involving the Union in conflicts outside the Western hemisphere. Such involvement would only lead the Union into an unending number of strenuous and devastating wars and conflicts, which, in their view, constitute a much greater threat to the United States. A significant aspect of this threat is that war waged in the name of national security usually leads to a curtailment of civil rights.

Developments in international relations leading up to the First World War had shown that the Monroe Doctrine could not be dogmatically upheld: under certain circumstances, the United States would be forced to intervene, politically and militarily, in conflicts outside the Western hemisphere, in defense of the national security of the Union. The questions of how and when this was to happen divided the American security establishment into, on the one hand, the missionaries, the revolutionary globalists, and, on the other, the warriors, the realist regionalists.[117] The first group wanted to make the world safe for democracy, because this really would be the only way to ensure the security of the nation. The second group wanted to make the United States safe for democracy, and only intervene militarily in the outside world when American security was faced with clear and serious threats. As long as conflicts did not immediately threaten American national security interests, international treaties, diplomacy and sanctions, backed by American military might, would suffice – in other words, the strategy which during the Cold War was summed up in the concepts of containment and deterrence. For the revolutionaries, a regime-change strategy which expands the number of democratic states is necessary; for the realists, democratic development is desirable, but cannot without considerable risk be forced through outside of the Western hemisphere.

This brings us to the division in the American political establishment prior to the invasion of Iraq in 2003, between those who were in favor of the war and those who opposed it. According to George W. Bush, and also particularly to his people at the Pentagon and associates of Vice President Dick Cheney, American security could only be ensured through the revolutionary regime-change strategy, which was first to be employed in the Middle East, more specifically in Iraq. They had in fact argued this point since 1996, when they were in opposition to the Clinton administration.[118] Their opponents did not disagree that Saddam Hussein was a bad guy, or that a regime change in Iraq as well as a democratization of the Middle East was desirable, but they felt that a war which had neither the justification of a clear, identifiable threat against U.S. national security nor any general international backing would produce more enemies than it might eliminate.

An evaluation of American Middle East policy thus largely depends on how the Middle East as a region is construed: is the Middle East a region similar to Eastern Europe, which would mean that the removal of despotic regimes can be expected to result in popular uprisings and demands for democratic rule? Or is the region so fundamentally different and poorly prepared for democracy that such intervention may lead to the opening of a Pandora's box of conflicts and problems, which will lead to widespread insecurity for many years to come?

The Democratic Deficit in the Middle East: Four Theories

The *Arab Human Development Report 2004*[119] establishes that, of the regions of the world, the Arab world suffers most severely from a democratic deficit, and that, at the same time, the populations in this region, compared with those in other regions, have the greatest degree of confidence in democratic rule. The observation that the Arab world is characterized by a democratic deficit is certainly not news. It is however a novel development that the West is making it a matter of international politics to amend that deficit. Although Bill Clinton made the promotion of democracy a central tenet of his conception of foreign policy, he made no real effort to promote democracy in the Arab world, but continued without the slightest sign of discomfort for instance to work closely together with Saudi Arabia. The EU attempted to link political reforms to economic aid through its Mediterranean policy – the Barcelona Process – but this did not constitute a concerted effort, and it had no consequences whatsoever for the policies towards those countries on the Arabian Peninsula which had not taken part in the process. Like the United States, the EU and Denmark turned a blind eye to the dictatorial conditions which dominated – and still dominate – in the Arab states in the Gulf.[120] As described in the above, this policy changed radically after September 11, 2001. Security is now to be based on the propagation of Western values, with the Middle East as the first target for this project. The Arab Initiative by the Danish Ministry of Foreign Affairs is a part of this new security policy.

In the literature on the Middle East, four main explanations for the democratic deficit in the Arab countries emerge. The first explanation considers the cultural tradition and Islam in particular to be the main stumbling block. The second one states that Western capitalism has systematically undermined the development of the region. The third explanation sees the Arab countries as *rentier* states, where highly centralist economies encourage clientalism and prevent popular participation in political decision-making processes. Finally, the fourth theory points out the fact that the Middle Eastern system of states was not, as in Europe, established through wars and power struggles, but was instead dictated by the Great Powers in connection with the peace negotiations following the First World War. Many accounts incorporate aspects of several of the theories. The four theories are briefly introduced in the following.

1. *The Explanation from Islamism*
According to a number of scholars such as Elie Kedourie and Bernard Lewis, as well as Danish commentators such as Ralf Pittelkow, the absence of democratic development is due to the fact that Islam is entirely incompatible with democracy, or to the fact that the Muslim countries have not undergone an Age of Enlightenment such as the European one.[121] These scholars point to the fact that democracy developed within Western civilization, and that among its prerequisites was the separation

between church and state which began early in European history, as well as the Reformation which meant that religion became a matter for the individual and, as such, something belonging to the private sphere. These developments were strengthened during the Enlightenment, where religion as tradition and scholarly field had to bear being discussed and examined on par with other societal and historical phenomena. This is the very tendency which, in the early 19th century, in the United States led to the establishment of Christian fundamentalism.[122] This movement was formed as an immediate reaction against the historicizing criticism of the Biblical text that characterizes modern Christian theology, which, according to fundamentalists, contributes to the subversion of the importance of Christian ethics in society and in everyday life. A similar battle over values regarding the interpretation of religion, it is maintained, has not taken place in the Islamic world – here, fundamentalism has remained unchallenged by enlightenment.

Islamists, as well as critics of Islam who argue that Islam is incompatible with democracy, often maintain that within Islam, religion and politics coincide. This is the Islamist interpretation, but within Islamic tradition, and seen from the perspective of history, religion and politics have in fact but rarely coincided. Far more common has been a separation between the executive branch of government and the Islamic authorities. This separation, secularization, seems more likely to be what the fundamentalists are reacting against. Rejecting the compatibility of Islam with democracy by citing the convergence of politics and religion within Islam amounts to giving primacy to the fundamentalist or Islamist construal of religion.

It is true that democracy as we currently understand it, meaning a political system including rights, duties, and an institutionalized guarantee that governments are made accountable for their actions through the possibility that they may be replaced in free and fair elections, developed in Europe rather than in the Orient. There are nonetheless quite a few examples of countries with Muslim populations which have practiced different forms of democracy. For instance India and Indonesia come to mind, and also Turkey, which, particularly under the Erdogan government which bases its politics on Islam, has demonstrated a willingness to introduce political reforms. Augustus Richard Norton, an American professor of international politics and Middle Eastern studies, in an article on this subject points out that many Muslims living in Western societies, such as Denmark, the Netherlands, the United States, France and the United Kingdom, have no problem maintaining their faith while adapting to the local democratic context. On the basis of comprehensive studies, French political scientist and Islam scholar Gilles Kepel even claims that the integration of European Muslims into Western political culture will contribute to democratic development in for instance South Asia and the Middle East. He contends that they will export their particular adaptation of Islam within European contexts to these parts of the world through the close ties they maintain with their home countries.[123] For generations now, we have certainly observed the development of an Islamic fundamentalism which opposes democracy. However, in Egypt, Lebanon, Jordan, Yemen, Algeria, Palestine, Tunisia and Morocco, we have also seen movements and parties based on Islam which have proved willing to participate in democratic processes. As a rule, though, these are categorically outlawed and barred from political decision-making processes by their respective governments – often, actually, with the explicit support of Western democracies. Islamic tradition, especially in the form of the development of Islamic fundamentalism which has been taking place for almost a century, seems to have significantly lacked democratic development. Yet it is obvious that fundamentalism does not in itself constitute the main cause of the democratic deficit, which cannot be explained by mere reference to the nature of Islam. In the same way, it would be wrong to claim that the New Testament provides the basis for and is the philosophical source of the Western liberal and democratic mode of government.

2. Dependency Theory

A second explanation is derived from so-called dependency theory.[124] While the explanation from Islamism primarily focuses on internal conditions, dependency theorists focus on external relations. They argue that capitalist development in the West, through exploitation and oppression, is responsible for systemic underdevelopment in the developing world. For economic reasons, the West, meaning the European powers, and later also the United States, have no interest in seeing the Arab nations undergo political and economic development. This is the primary cause of the democratic deficit. While a number of poignant examples exist and may be brought forth to substantiate this argument, one might also point out an obvious weakness of this theory: a number of countries in the so-called third world have actually managed to develop into democracies and to create economic progress. Dependency theory fails to explain why the state of affairs in the Arab countries is different from those in other developing countries. And while global capitalism is certainly problematic in many ways, and responsible for a lot of problems as far as the relationship between the northern and southern hemispheres is concerned, it cannot in and of itself be considered solely responsible for the lack of democracy in the Middle East.

3. *The Arab Rentier State*

In a series of major works and articles, the economist Giacomo Luciani has developed the concept of the rentier state.[125] He points out that in Arab states the public sector is typically far too large compared to the gross national product. This is borne out even in comparisons with non-Arab countries with comparable economies. This is particularly true with respect to oil rich states in the Gulf, where quite significant oil revenues have been invested in infrastructure, education, health and the establishment and maintenance of state enterprises. The income of these states has been obtained through oil exports rather than through taxation. Correspondingly, the private sectors are small. However, in all these countries, considerable informal or even illegal economic activity takes place. The economic structure is thus made up of a combination of large, inefficient public sectors and a widespread grey or black market. In the Gulf, political rights have typically been traded in for welfare benefits provided by the state, according to the motto of *no taxation, no representation.* According to Luciani and other scholars, the rentier state promotes and perpetuates cliental structures, in which the state bargains with for instance the bourgeoisie over rights and privileges instead of implementing actual reforms. Several scholars emphasize that this clientalism in the Arab world thrives in traditional tribal, clan and family structures. This was especially obvious in Iraq under Saddam Hussein during the period of sanctions, where an actual refeudalization was said to have taken place. Once more, it may be pointed out that the phenomenon of the rentier state is not exclusive to the Arab world, but also occurs elsewhere and as a result of dissimilar kinds of development. While the theory of the rentier state undoubtedly contributes to an explanation of why certain Arab countries have not developed into democracies, it does not represent a full explanation.

4. The Explanation from History

The American political scientist and Middle East scholar Ian Lustic has pointed out that, from the vantage point of history, there is nothing unusual about Iraq's 1991 attempt at solving her financial and national security problems through war and the occupation of Kuwait. The European system of states was in fact established on the basis of wars. What was unusual in the case of Iraq was that Iraq was not allowed to carry out this plan. This is of course due to the dramatic changes which the international political system has undergone after the two world wars, and particularly with the establishment of the UN system, the whole point of which was to prevent wars of aggression between sovereign states. At a time when the European and Western system of states through innumerable wars had acquired a relatively stable balance of power, an international system was established which severely limited the ability of other regions to establish their balance of power through war. The result of the European history of wars was the formation of a system of nation states, within which national identity and state borders largely coincided.

This has not been the case in the Middle East. Certainly the formation of the states resulted from a war, the First World War, but the borders were drawn by the Great Powers and the victors. Up until the Treaty of Versailles no Arab states existed, only provinces under the Ottoman Empire. They were not precisely delimited, and neither the new borders which were drawn by France, the United Kingdom and Italy nor those already in existence reflected what might be termed natural boundaries or divisions along the lines of ethnic, cultural and religious identity structures. They merely reflected the distribution of the interests of the Great Powers. In a series of studies of political and national identity in the Arab and Middle Eastern state system, the British Middle East scholar and Syria expert Raymond Hinnebusch has been prominent in demonstrating certain consequences of this artificial drawing of state borders – sometimes referred to as 'lines in the sand': the new Arab governments have been settled with a number of challenges in the form of a dilemma. On the one hand, they must govern heterogenous and composite populations, characterized by groups which identify themselves on the basis of ethnic and religious affiliations as well as transnational identity such as pan-Arabism and pan-Islamism. On the other hand, they are faced with the demands and expectations of the international system that they must act as representatives for stable and sovereign nation states.[126]

As a result of this dilemma, certain governments have legitimized themselves by shuttling between a transnational identity – as when President Nasser of Egypt attempted to establish an Arab union and a united front against Israel – and a fight for the national interests of the state, which has often contradicted the transnational identity, as when Egypt made a separate peace with Israel at the 1978 Camp David Accords. This resulted not only in the division between the Arab countries which isolated Egypt, but also in a division within Egypt, where the Islamic opposition identified more with the Muslim brothers in Palestine, Jordan, Lebanon and Syria than with the Egyptian state. This is why the state, after a short period under the leadership of Anwar Sadat, has suppressed the country's Islamic opposition movements – a brutal policy which has received the support of Western democracies.

These dilemmas and contradictions inherent in the construction of national identity in the Arab countries have been used by the regimes in their efforts to explain why political reforms will lead to instability, dissolution and conflict rather than progress, peace and stability. This has all contributed to creating an image of the Arab world as a region of unrest and internal conflict, which can only be controlled through the maintenance of authoritarian regimes. This understanding is not restricted to the Arab regimes themselves, but has received widespread Western support. As a case in point, no interest was shown in removing Saddam Hussein after the Gulf War in 1991, because it was assumed that this would only lead to a violent civil war. In a similar manner a blind eye was turned to the internal conditions in the Gulf states and Egypt.[127] With respect to the Gulf states, this was due to the fact that they were providers of oil and also represented a lucrative market, which it was feared might be lost due to internal conflicts. As far as Egypt was concerned, bordering Palestine and at peace with Israel she might play a helpful role in the peace process, which could not be risked in a perilous process of political reform. Western governments preferred to listen to President Hosni Mubarak's explanation; that Egypt was not yet ready for democracy.[128] In the 2005 UNDP report, this type of policy is quite fittingly referred to as *blackmail of legitimacy*. Arab regimes as well as Western Middle East policy preferred authoritarian rule and stability over political reform and instability, up until September 11, 2001, when the actions of Osama bin Laden and his operatives changed the minds of the United States and the EU. As publicly acknowledged by George W. Bush in his famous November 2003 speech, Western democracies bear part of the responsibility for the democratic deficit presently characterizing the Arab world.

Universalism or Regionalism?

The British political scientist and Middle East scholar Fred Halliday has suggested that the field of Middle East studies is largely divided into two camps: one group, the universalists, employ universal theories on issues such as development, modernity, and international economics in their analysis of Middle Eastern affairs, without taking particular regional and cultural circumstances into account. The other group, the regionalists, takes a contrary approach: they emphasize particular regional conditions, particularly cultural ones, in explaining why regions develop differently.[129] If we consider the four theories previously introduced, dependency theory can be termed a universalist theory, which exactly highlights its weakness: if the theory is correct, then how can it be that some developing countries have become democratic while others have not? The explanation from Islam is a regionalist theory, which also constitutes its weakness: how can it be that Islam is a hindrance to the development of democracy in some places, but not in others? The theory of the rentier state as well as the explanation from history combine the regional with universal theories – albeit in different ways. The explanation from history focuses on ideological matters, while the theory of the rentier state finds its explanation in matters of economy. According to Halliday's subdivision, then, the theory of the rentier state leans towards universalism, while the explanation from history leans towards regionalism. Nonetheless they both approximate Halliday's own ideal that Middle East research – and area studies in general – must necessarily combine analytical universalism with historical particularism. Wherever one stands on this issue, it is interesting to note that the political actors in their strategies of legitimization make much use of the available theories, which will be apparent from the historical examples to which we now turn.

Middle Eastern Globalization Strategies

The people rises up, sheds the yoke, exiles the dictators, and democracy replaces years of oppression by authoritarian regimes. This would appear to be the underlying narrative of the enthusiasm surrounding the tide of democracy which has swept the Arab world since the war in Iraq: the presidential election in Palestine and the elections in Iraq, demonstrations in Lebanon, local elections in Saudi Arabia, and minor reform measures in connection with the 2005 parliamentary elections in Egypt which allowed more candidates to participate. This narrative is inspired by the struggle of Eastern European nations for freedom during and after the final breaths of the Soviet empire, which resulted in the so-called velvet revolutions. The images of East Germans literally breaking down the Berlin Wall, or of the masses taking to the streets and demanding their freedom in the capitals of Eastern Europe, remain fresh in the minds of many. Whether popular movements and sentiment actually were instrumental in bringing about democracy is, however, questionable. Upon his long heralded death, Pope John Paul II was hailed as the man who broke the back of Communism. Previously this honor – especially on the occasion of his death – had been bestowed upon Ronald Reagan. Elsewhere, people such as the Czech Vaclav Havel and the Pole Lech Walesa are considered important figures. In Russia, the legacy of Mikhail Gorbachev as the man whose reforms brought down the Communist house of cards is the object of both admiration and skepticism. Even though democracy means the rule of the people, its implementation is not unequivocally a matter for the people. At the very least, there is more to it. The storming of the Bastille would never have taken place had not a bourgeois elite spearheaded the revolution. And was it not a king who gave the Danes their constitution? In the United States it is not the populace but rather the Founding Fathers who are referred to when the freedom of the American Union is celebrated. Elites and rulers, even kings and princes, have contributed in the establishment of the free world, and there is no reason to believe that this should be any different in the Middle East. Disregarding for a moment the fact that the significance of the tide of democracy which is now sweeping the Arab world can be called into question, it is appropriate to note that the processes of reform we are indeed witnessing are only to a limited extent the achievement of the people – though they will hopefully soon benefit the Arab peoples. This is true in the case of Yemen as well as with regard to other Arab nations in the Gulf. Throughout the Arabian Peninsula, reforms which aim at widening the access to the processes of political decision making are actually created by the governing regimes.

At this point, an objection may be made that the fact that the processes of reform originate with the regimes rather than with the populace results from the continued insistence of the regimes on their total control of the political process, a state of affairs which does not allow for the implementation of popular rule. This is unquestionably true. Yet the question still remains whether democratization would be furthered if the regimes were to loosen controls and allow the people to be heard through free and fair elections. Although Danish and American Middle East policies aim at popular rule or democracy, as expressed in 'The Arab Initiative' and the United States' 'Greater Middle East Project,' it remains highly doubtful whether free elections at the present time would serve to achieve this goal. Rather, the risk seems to be that the contrary might occur, with anti-democratic forces in fact gaining access to power.

Yemen and Saudi Arabia

We are faced, then, with a dilemma: the processes of reform currently introduced by the regimes are narrowly regulated and lead merely to a very restricted form of 'democracy,' as seen in Yemen, or to mockeries of elections like the 2005 Saudi local elections – while a fully democratic process risks leading to new dictatorships or worse. In other words, the dilemma seems to consist in a choice between strictly controlled reforms or chaos.

Nothing is entirely clear-cut. In Yemen a more open and less heavily controlled political process *might* have led to genuine democratization. The political reform process in this area began with the unification of North and South Yemen in 1990. Heading the new republic was the

The Democratic Dilemma

Since the unification of North and South Yemen in 1990, a number of elections have been held in the new republic. Seen here are banners flown during the 2003 election campaign.

president of the former North Yemen, Ali Abdullah Saleh, who had been in power there since 1978. Since 1990, Saleh's leadership has led to a greater integration of the Yemenite state, and a process of political reform has been implemented which has led to political pluralism; three parliamentary elections as well as one presidential election and a referendum on the constitution have been held, all designated as relatively free by international observers. These developments notwithstanding, it is quite obvious that the aim of Saleh's policy is to secure all political power for himself and his party, the General People's Congress.

Initially, the aim was to create alliances which would facilitate the unification and the establishment of the Republic of Yemen in 1990. As part of this process, the president cooperated with the socialist elite in the South, but after it had been completed, Saleh needed to marginalize the socialists. For this purpose he allied himself with one of the Northern tribal associations, the *Hashid,* which is led by Sheikh Abdullah al-Ahmar, who was later to head *Islah*, the Sunni reform party. Soon after the unification, however, tensions between Salah's North Yemen and the socialists in the South began to grow, with mysterious assassinations of leading figures becoming the order of the day. Things came to a head with the 1994 civil war, in which Saleh was supported by the *Islah*, significantly including the Afghanistan veteran Sheikh Abdullah al-Majid al-Zindani, reportedly an acquaintance of Osama bin Laden. Zindani has long been known as a most active supporter of the Salafists. Politically, these belong to the extremist wing of *Islah.* In a dedicated and often violent campaign, they disseminate their brand of Islam through numerous private religious institutes.[130] These institutes, many of which are based on Salafism, have grown in number after the return of almost 800,000 Yemenites to Yemen in the early 1990s. Some of these were ejected from Saudi Arabia, which refused to renew their work permits because Yemen supported Iraq in the conflict over Kuwait. Others returned from the battlefields of Afghanistan upon the completion of their Jihad against the Soviet forces, which were withdrawn from Afghanistan in 1989. In Saudi Arabia as well as in Afghanistan some of them had been inspired by Salafism, and it was with their help that President Saleh managed to marginalize the socialists and destroy their party organization, whose possessions and capital were confiscated after the civil war, while its leaders were sent into exile.

Islah took over the role as the second largest party in the Yemenite parliament, and was, in the local communities of the Aden and Abyan provinces, able to fill the gap left by the socialists. But by the time of the 1997 parliamentary elections, it was *Islah*'s turn to be pushed aside. This effort has also met with success, as Saleh's General People's Congress now rules supreme in the capital of Sanaa. But the process has met with its share of resistance, and has resulted in a marked radicalization of parts of the *Islah* as well as of other Islamist groups, who have been subjected to pressure by Saleh. It is from among these groups that the Aden-Abyan Islamic Army does its recruiting – an organization which has carried out a number of bombings in Yemen, and which achieved infamy with the 1998 kidnapping of 16 Western tourists. During that episode, four tourists were killed when Yemenite government troops attempted to free the hostages. During the aftermath it was revealed that the group had connections to radical Islamist groups centered around the Finsbury Park Mosque in London.

The United States places Zindani in connection with al-Qaida as well as with the 2000 bombing of the American destroyer USS Cole, and has consequently called for his arrest. So far, Yemen has merely restricted him from leaving the country – a fact which is criticized in the report on global terrorism issued by the American State Department in April 2005.[131] The Yemenites display an ambiguous attitude. In cooperation with the United States, and with a complete disregard for civil rights, individuals and groups accused of terrorist activity are mercilessly pursued and punished. This has recently led to violent clashes in the northern part of the country, resulting in almost 400 deaths and thousands of refugees. Meanwhile, the Islamists are allowed to dominate the religious institutes. Overall, a picture emerges of precarious double-dealing kept up by the president, who juggles different alliances in his effort to maintain his monopoly on power: on the one hand, the *Islah* has been forced into opposition; on the other hand, Ali Abdullah Saleh manages to keep a straight face while allowing the establishment of institutions inspired by Salafism.[132]

Prospects were promising when the Republic of Yemen was established, got a free constitution, and held a referendum as well as parliamentary elections. It could have led to political pluralism and democracy. Instead, the president has used the elections in his effort to monopolize power

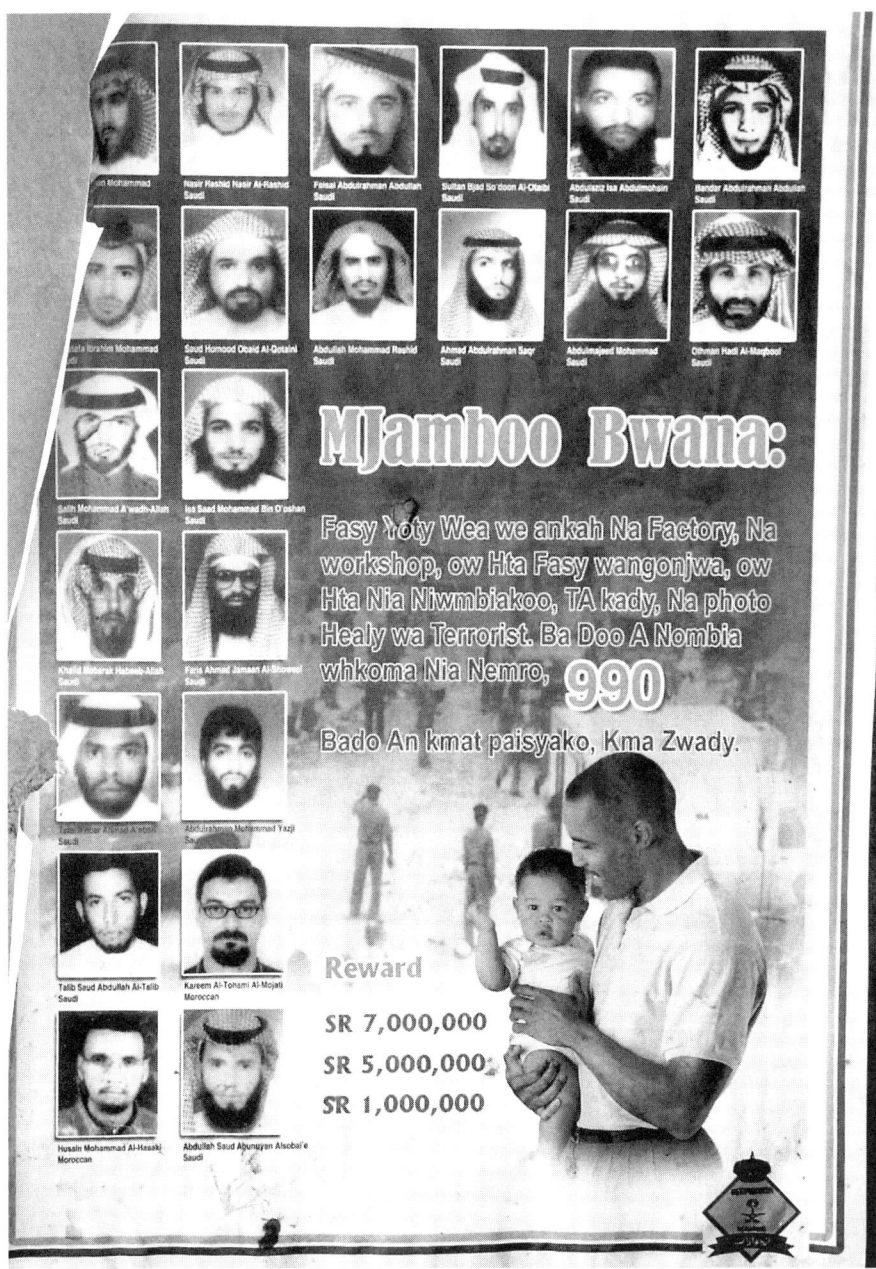

Since the onset of al-Qaida terrorist activities, Saudi Arabia has commenced a widespread hunt for terrorists. Posters depicting wanted individuals are displayed, as during the German hunt for Rote Arme terrorists. Because Saudi Arabia imports much of its workforce from Asia, the messages must be translated into many different languages. This poster was displayed in the Jeddah marketplace.

and marginalize the opposition. As a result, groups of frustrated and disappointed activists abound from which militant Islamists can easily obtain new recruits.[133]

In Saudi Arabia it seems that opposition to the royal family was propagated and became solidly manifested through the success of Islamic fundamentalists in local elections. These fundamentalists are not in favor of 'Westernization' or democratization; on the contrary, they are highly critical of the royal family's close relationship with the West. For Islamic scholars in Saudi Arabia who command a popular following, a government based solely on Islamic law, rather than democracy, is seen as the proper course. Local council candidates who enjoyed the backing of these scholars were the most successful among male voters in local elections (women were not allowed to vote). Widespread sympathy with the Islamist doctrine of Osama bin Laden exists within Saudi society. The royal family's manner of practising Islam, once derided as 'American Islam' by Osama bin Laden, is also widely opposed. Consequently, it cannot be ruled out that free elections in Saudi Arabia might lead to a government modelled on the Afghan Taliban regime rather than on that very epitome of freedom, the United States of America wish for.

Algerian Prelude

Reforms, democratic developments and free elections have been known to provide Islamists with considerable popular following. This happened in connection with the Algerian local elections in 1990, with the parliamentary elections in 1991, and, had the second round been carried out in January 1992, it would have led to a considerable majority for the Islamic fundamentalists in the Algerian Parliament. This development was halted by a military coup, alleviating concerns of European as well as American politicians. The extremely bloody civil war which followed did, however, rattle the otherwise staunch resolve of Washington and Brussels, and members of the Bush administration then in power, including James Baker, later regretted their support for the military coup.[134] While supporting military coups certainly is out of tune with Western governments' policy of exporting democracy, there is no way of knowing what the ramifications of an Islamic fundamentalist government in Algeria might have been. It is, however, almost unimaginable that such a government would have preserved a newfound democracy.[135] Perhaps the lessons of

Algeria have played a part in creating the peculiar current strategy of Western politicians: on the one hand, they give opulent rhetorical praise to the project of the new American order of introducing democracy in the Middle East, while, on the other hand, quietly accepting narrowly controlled processes of reform as a start towards achieving the objective. Perhaps this strategy is actually quite wise. Perhaps it would be even wiser to tone down the moral vision of free elections as the symbol of the new order, and concentrate instead on rights and due process of law as the material from which the road to a safer and better life for Middle Eastern populations must be built. But the Western policy which, on the one hand, encourages free elections but, on the other, supports military coups when these elections yield results considered undesirable by the West, sends out seriously ambiguous messages; it involves the West in the Middle Eastern battle over values in a way which casts doubt upon the true content of the Western model of society: Western economic and security interests, or rights for everyone irrespective of religious or ethnic affiliation.

Anti-Western Opposition
There are several reasons for the strong resistance currently emerging against the efforts of the Americans and their allies to implement democracy in the Middle East.

Firstly, there is the problem posed by what can be termed the double-entry book keeping of the West: why is it so urgent that Arabs and Muslims abide by international law, when the United States and Israel are exempt? This is a question frequently asked in the Middle East. Taking this problem into account, efforts to implement the American order in accordance with the Western interpretation of freedom ring hollow – they are seen as a way for the West to gain control of the Middle East. In Arab coffee shops, the question is posed of why Westerners refrain from demanding that Israel abide by UN resolutions? This was demanded of Saddam Hussein, and is currently demanded of Syria. Why did the Syrian military presence in Lebanon constitute a problem, when the Israeli presence in a smaller part of Lebanon and in much of Palestine do not? The answer is that Israel, unlike Syria, is a democracy. But if that is the real reason, then why does the West support undemocratic regimes such as those in Saudi Arabia and Egypt?

Secondly, there is the coupling of war and morality, which most nearly resembles the medieval notion of just war. Today, the United States and the West wage war under the auspices of humanity, while in the Middle Ages, it was done in the name of Christianity and the Church. And those who oppose the Western interpretation of humanity and freedom are sinners – or, in the oft repeated words of George W. Bush, 'bad guys'. As was true for Medieval Christians, different rules apply with regard to those who favor humanism and those who oppose it.

Under the authority of the Holy See, enemies who were of the Christian persuasion were able to expect and demand that wars waged against them were conducted in accordance with certain rules, laws and treaties – and that once war was over, a peace could be negotiated. As far as non-Christians were concerned, however, no rules applied. They were to be either Christianized or annihilated – on the assumption that if they did not receive the Christian message, they must have no souls, and were therefore by definition not a part of the human community. This line of thought was formulated by one of the original European authors of international law, Francisco de Vitoria, in his treatise on the conduct of the Spanish *conquistadores* towards the natives of the New World.[136]

Similar notions are picked up on by many in the Arab world, in connection with the so-called war on terror – as stated by Bush in September 2001: "Either you are with us, or you are with the terrorists." The terrorists – 'the bad guys' – are, as 'enemies of humanity,' opposed to the Western interpretation of freedom and humanity, and do therefore not qualify as human beings to whom the same rights can be ascribed as those that apply to criminals who can be prosecuted according to the civilian code of penal law. Neither do they qualify as soldiers (prisoners of war), who must be treated in accordance with the Geneva Conventions; they are defined as 'enemy combatants,' without the civil rights applicable to Western citizens, and may thus be detained at Guantanamo. And if keeping them there should become too troublesome, they may be transported by means of secret CIA flights – so-called 'renditions' – to for instance secret prison camps in Afghanistan, where they are effectively detained in 'no man's land.' All of this takes place with the tacit approval of European democracies.

This battle between the good guys and the bad guys, between the disciples of freedom and the forces of darkness, waged by the West as 'the war on terror' (with the support of regimes in Pakistan, Saudi Arabia, Afghanistan, Yemen and Algeria, because it provides them with an opportunity to rid themselves of certain enemies), is seen by many in the Middle East as the Holy War of the West against Muslims. In their view, the problem is that war conducted in the name of humanity defines the opponent as non-human and without rights. This is a war without clear delimitations – and, oddly, though it is meant to promote democracy, humanism and human rights, it employs a systematic disregard for due legal process, human rights and human life. This is a war which is constantly producing new enemies; enemies who are puzzled by the fact that they have been excluded from the humanity which the war proclaims to defend.

Thirdly, the Arab governments, more often than not with the support of the West and the United States, have prevented popular participation in political decision-making processes, and have zealously removed and eliminated any opposition. This has taken place in many different ways and with the employment of many different sets of references. In Saudi Arabia, the regime has maintained an Islamic principle of unity (tawhid), which has consistently become institutionalized in Saudi society through an almost totalitarian monitoring and regulation of everything from the educational system to gyms and public spaces like the streets and shop interiors. The opposition to secularization and Americanized Islam which is widespread among the Saudi population is due to the effectiveness of indoctrination: the socialization into Wahhabist Islam has succeeded to an extent which makes it difficult for the Saudi Arabian government to implement reforms. In other words, the society which the Saudi state has created through violence and coercion, with a view to securing order and control over the largest oil reserve in the world, is now the source of the greatest resistance to reforms. Even if the royal family in Riyadh had learned the lesson of the West and decided to turn the country into a democracy tomorrow, the reaction of the people would not be in favor of democracy, but rather in favor of Islamism, which might well lead to the country's falling apart. Saudi Arabian investments in the United States worth 600 billion dollars would be lost, and a global economic crisis would result from skyrocketing oil prices of up to $150 per barrel.[137] The American administration therefore welcomes the Saudi contribution to the war against 'bad guys' – irrespec-

The Democratic Dilemma

Since the Second World War, the United States and Saudi Arabia have maintained a close relationship. This relationship is still cultivated. Here, the American Secretary of State Condoleezza Rice visits with then Crown Prince Abdullah, in Riyadh, in June 2005. Abdullah was appointed King on August 1, 2005.

tive of the fact that it is conducted without the least trace of respect for the rule of law. The recent local elections are therefore emphasized as a democratic beginning, because taking it further would risk the collapse of the Saudi Arabian kingdom and an attendant global economic crisis on par with the depression of the 1930s. And this accurately presents the background for the suspicion towards the well-meaning Western democratization projects in the Middle East permeating large parts of the Arab populations: it seems that Western freedom only extends as far as the economic stability of the Western world.

Dubai: Fenced-In Globalization and Cultural Apartheid

Paths other than the 'fake' democracy of Yemen and the 'wannabe'-totalitarianism of Saudi Arabia have been chosen by other states which are less closely watched by ever-vigilant Western media. Dubai, the second largest of the United Arab Emirates, has chosen a strategy which balances between fenced-in globalization and cultural apartheid. In recognition of the fact that the oil revenues of the Emirate are not a perpetual source of wealth, the Emir family has initiated a strategy of securing future wealth through foreign investments: the more foreign capital the better. This began in the early 1990s with the establishment of the *Jebel Ali Free Zone*. The plan, which succeeded, was to make Dubai attractive to foreign investments by creating an exception from the GCC (Gulf Cooperation Council) rule which limits the ownership of foreign companies to 49 percent within the region. Within the free zone, anyone who so desired was allowed to own up to 100 percent. At the same time, Dubai opened up to investments into all kinds of facilities, such as office complexes, hotels, exclusive beaches, fancy golf resorts and a large shopping facility which would service business executives and attract tourists. Tourism in itself became a sector capable of attracting foreign capital. Dubai thus became a new center for globalization, which increasingly emerged as a free-for-all for exorbitant projects and investments. The success has led to new projects such as the building of artificial islands, in order that wealthy global citizens may purchase their own little islands on which to build their castles. Although this is indeed a free-for-all, as long as projects are extravagant and expensive, the Emir family is making sure that what goes on is in keeping with its construal of modern consumer culture: while prospectuses speak of 'Culture in Diversity,' all the pictures show huge white houses, with design furnishings, grand pianos and ocean views – and a Porsche frequently comes with the purchase of an estate. With a view to ensuring that the new inhabitants of Dubai's artificial islands continue to desire the refreshment of a dive into the bay waters along their estates, the contractor dumps a kilo of gold into the water on a daily basis. This is supposed to further motivate taking an exclusive dive, in case fatigue sets in at the end of a long day of million dollar deals in the Jebel Ali Free Zone and the subsequent relaxing long drink on the artificial island terrace.

Visiting Dubai, one is confronted with a hyperactive society: homes and hotels are constructed at a speed which by comparison would make Miami Beach in Florida seem like a Copenhagen suburb. *Media City*, which houses all the major global media corporations, and *Education City*, which attracts foreign universities, are both expanding at a pace more reminiscent of aggressive cancer cell development than of regulated city planning. Throughout the 1990s, Dubai has developed into the playground of globalization *par excellence*, and signs are few and far between that the country is actually run by an autocratic Emir family, and that it is in fact an Arab, Muslim nation.

Although local leaders are constantly referred to and depicted in the media, very few locals are visible in the streetscape of Dubai. They remain hidden away behind the walls of ostentatious palaces which may only be viewed from the outside – except by individuals of particular economic or political importance, such as the American national security advisor or Bill Gates, the founder of Microsoft. Visitors may of course happen upon locals who do not enjoy the privilege of belonging to the inner circle of the Emir family. These, however, will often merely be hanging about, looking important – they most certainly do not work! The relatively ordinary locals show up in the street mainly to observe the advent of globalization in the desert state, to seduce Western beauties, or to lecture male occidentals and ignorant fools on the topic of the true and the right. Mainly, however, they come to consume. Whenever we happen upon one of the locals wearing the local 'outfit,' we are pleased finally to be able to learn something about the place, but each time we are reminded that for every uniformed police officer, five plain clothed ones are hanging around, and this person may very well be one of them.

When encountering a local person at the bank, at the office building or in the bar, he turns out – for it is always a 'he' – to be as much of a tourist or visitor as we are. He has made his way into the multicultural realm of Dubai, but remains in perpetual retreat into the pristine and virginal *hinterland* beyond the invisible cultural fence which sharply separates them from us.

Two separate narratives are employed in the self-promoting efforts of the Emir family. One describes Dubai as the center of globalization. This is substantiated by a hotel boasting no less than seven stars, the construction of the world's tallest skyscraper, and most exclusive golf courses, the annual upkeep of which is unbelievably costly because they happen to be laid out in the desert. This narrative aims at attracting foreign investments. The other narrative takes the form of a national myth, which describes the Emir family as the protector of Arab tradition

Artificial islands, seven-star hotels, and the world's tallest skyscraper are to ensure Dubai's first class seat on the globalization train. The intended height of the skyscraper is kept secret by the Emir family, but it is estimated that it will be more than 700 meters tall, at a cost of more than $870 million.

and Islamic ethics. It serves to legitimize the regime to the locals, who today constitute a mere 10 percent of the inhabitants of the United Arab Emirates – the remaining 90 percent is made up by foreign workers, who do not tire the Emir with annoying requests that they be afforded rights. Sheikh Zayed bin Sultan al-Nahyan, until his death in 2004 the unchallenged leader of the Union, is represented in the myth as the righteous, generous, wise man who wandered in from the desert, where he had served as a role model in his conduct of the traditional activities of Bedouin life, such as falconry and camel breeding. The myth is documented by museums and cultural cities, representing the proud and virtuous Arab way of life. Today, this way of life is conducted in the privacy of the home, and this where the cultural onward movement of globalization is halted. Outside these walls, Western consumers may romp and roam to their hearts' desire, as long as they spend money in the country. They are denied access behind these walls, and on the rare occasion when they do gain access, they must leave their cultural trappings outside. Non-Muslims are not allowed inside mosques in the United Arab Emirates, with the exception of a single one, to which entry tickets may be acquired that allow sneak peaks for a couple of hours each week – if one can get one's hands on these tickets, of course. Like tiny authentic, pristine islands, surrounded by the artificial consumer paradises of globalization, Arab and Muslim identity must prevail, pure and untainted. As an example of the zeal of the Emir family when it comes to the prevention of the cultural bastardization of the locals, it will pay upwards of 70,000 dollars to local men upon their first marriage to a local girl – mixed marriages are frowned upon.

How does this fenced-in policy of globalization and cultural apartheid lead to reforms? Only in the sense that it creates a huge private sector, which over the years has gained influence over economic policy. This does not constitute democracy, but it does open up limited areas of the decision-making processes. In this way, the Emir family manages to retain their power and control, ensure continued growth even after the oil wells have dried up, while also preserving the local cultural identity. But the project depends entirely on the continued patronage and investments of wealthy world citizens and corporations. As long as this continues, the fiction of multicultural consumption prevails in Dubai – for now.

Qatar: Elitist Reform Process

The neighboring emirate of Qatar represents an alternative model. Qatar is the home of the *al-Jazeera* satellite television station, and also played host to the headquarters of the American Army during the Iraq war in 2003. Although the Emir of Qatar also seeks to attract foreign investments, and has supported the development of a private sector, which is meant to secure Qatar's share of the fruits of globalization, a quite different strategy is employed here. Since the Emir assumed power in a palace coup in 1995, the project of modernization has run parallel to a project of reform in education, which aims at making the Qataris the best educated population in the Gulf, as well as at turning the jobs held by foreign workers over to the local population. Up until 1995, Qatar could be considered a kind of miniature Saudi Arabia, with similar ideology and type of government. In Qatar the educational system was likewise dominated by the doctrine of Wahhabism, which allowed for no critical or political reflection. Political opening has taken place since 1995, and in 2003, a referendum was held concerning a new constitution which is supposed to pave the way for a parliamentary system. Yet the same problems which, though on a much larger scale, make political reform very difficult in Saudi Arabia, are also present here. As in Saudi Arabia, in Qatar the policy of reform is met with the greatest resistance among the populace, which continues to comply with traditional Islamic values as interpreted by Wahhabism. This is why the decommissioning of the traditional and strictly controlled Qatari educational system is at the top of the list of priorities of the reform policy.

This process of modernization was initiated in 1995, but has now been launched in earnest, in connection with a project which aims at reforming the entire educational system, from the primary school level to the university level. Critical reflection, dialogue and discussion skills, modern knowledge and, of course, a prioritization of skills in the areas of natural science and technology are key aspects of this reconfiguration of the educational system. It seems obvious that these tacit adjustments in due course will lead to secularization, and that, in the long term, it will create an educated population which will demand political influence and be prepared to participate in an open political process.

The reforms initiated by the Emir, who retains the imposing status of autocratic prince, will eventually subvert the basis for his own authority.

However, this seem to be the intention, based on the assumption that this is the only way for Qatar to secure its future prosperity and role in a globalized world. Instead of cultural apartheid and fenced-in globalization, the Emir of Qatar thus heads an elitist process of reform, which will in the near future have created a popular basis for the actual democratization of the country. Whether this will actually happen remains to be seen, but these are promising perspectives compared to the ones characterizing Saudi Arabia and the United Arab Emirates. However, it will be some time before critical reflection can be unfolded in discussions at the University of Qatar: a professor who showed his students *Jyllands-Posten*'s Muhammad drawings was immediately dismissed. This clearly indicates that the battle over values between Islam and political life still dominate the Qatari reform process.

Are All People Equal?

Yemen, Qatar and Dubai have all turned their backs on Saudi Arabia in their choice of development models. They have, however, each done so in their own way: Yemen has chosen a pluralist political system based on a free constitution; while this resembles a democratization, it is actually exclusively controlled by the serving president, who completely monopolizes political and economic power. In Dubai, the strategy still consists in withholding political influence from the people, which is compensated by the securing of tax-free growth and prosperity. In Qatar, the Emir has launched an elitist process of reform which – provided it is continued – will pave the way for a modern, regular democracy.

The securing of basic rights for the population is problematic in all of these countries, including Saudi Arabia. In all four countries, human rights violations are the order of the day, and due process is far from being a given. Unfortunately, the disregard of rights in these countries is exacerbated by the war on terror, the hunt for 'bad guys.' Unfortunately the West, led by the United States, turns a blind eye to this disregard of rights, as long as it is taking place in the holy name of the war on terror. This subverts Western assurances that the true purpose of the war against terrorism and the war in Iraq is to bring freedom and democracy to the Middle East. Keeping in mind Guantanamo, Abu Ghraib and the illegitimate American prison camps in Afghanistan, it seems that Kant was right in predicting that the wars waged by democracies against non-democratic regimes would be brutal and conducted with disregard for international rules of war. These circumstance lend credibility to the concerns of the realist regionalists that the revolutionary regime-change strategy in the Middle East in fact creates more enemies than it removes. Perhaps it would be wiser to end the talk of freedom and democracy, and leave it to the Arabs themselves to search out viable models of political development of their own?

Rather than focusing on the exportation of democracy, the West might insist on a comprehensive, worldwide adherence to basic rights – also in the pursuit of terrorists, who may well be 'bad guys' but who are, first and foremost, political agents, employing illegitimate means within illegitimate, authoritarian societies. Perhaps the West would meet with greater understanding among Arab peoples if it was to insist that the rights ascribed to their own citizens be likewise ascribed to political opponents, including those who, entirely unacceptably, make use of terrorism in their political struggle. Perhaps it might even facilitate democracy in the Middle East if the West was to tone down its moral ambition and fairly regard conflicts in the Middle East, not as conflicts between the disciples of freedom and the lords of darkness, but as political conflicts which can only be solved politically, under condition of respect for the rights to which we consider ourselves entitled. The strategy of the revolutionary globalists, then, consists in the forced implementation of democracy in the Middle East, facilitated by their refraining from demanding the democratization of the Arab states and settling for fake reforms, as for instance in Yemen and Saudi Arabia. Meanwhile, they continue their cooperation with these states in the war on terror, thereby ignoring systematic rights violations. If this strategy is allowed to continue, the realist regionalists will likely have predicted correctly that the war on terror in the name of democracy does in fact create more enemies than it removes.

So far, our analysis has focused on the war on terror and its ramifications in terms of the global battle over values between Islamism and Western order. Besides the existence of widespread mistrust of the United States and Western policies towards the Middle East and Asia, as well as frustration and anger at political developments after 9/11, which in themselves serve to strengthen Islamist opposition, militant Islamists have intensified the conflict by responding with still more terrorist attacks and support for the armed insurgency in Iraq and Afghanistan. The next section focuses on the Islamic based terrorism of al-Qaida, and examines its development from being an organisation of experienced jihadists to becoming a strategy employed by local, inexperienced, small groups, like the one responsible for the July 2005 London bombings.

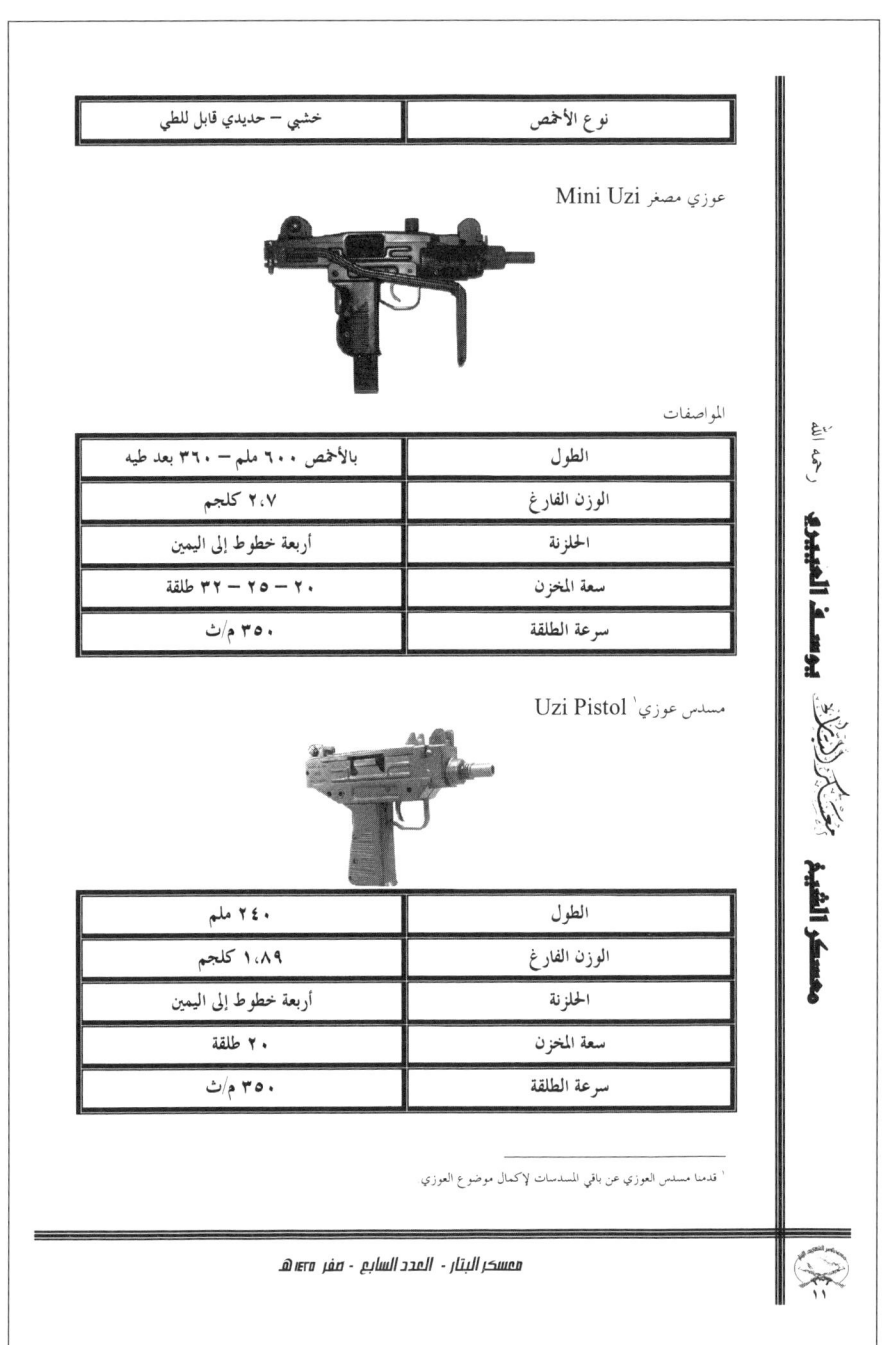

An introduction to the UZI submachine gun, taken from the Saudi Jihad periodical al-Battar. Cf. Part 3 of this book, as well as the photo caption on page 152.

Part 3
The Globalization of Al-Qaida's Battle over Values

They can take away our freedom in the streets and in the mosques, but we are still free on the Internet.

Today, it is our way of thinking which is received and shows itself to be stronger than yours. Islam rest safely on a God, a Prophet, a Koran and a tradition. This creates hatred in the mind of the West, and, realizing that it has lost, it resorts to violence and war against Islam.

The spreading of democracy is just an excuse. Just as the hunt for Osama bin Laden is an excuse. It is Islam itself which is anathema to Western thinking, and this is how these events must be understood. The assault on Islam is like a hand: One finger is the war in Iraq and Afghanistan. The other finger is the detainment of Muslims at Guantanamo. The third is the publication of the drawings of the Prophet Muhammad. We have to see things for what they are, and the drawings are a part of the West's militant battle against Islam.

Interview with Mullah Krekah, *Dagbladet* (Oslo), March 13, 2006

Al-Qaida: From Organization to Ideology

The hijackers who carried out the September 11, 2001 attacks on New York and Washington were all of Middle Eastern descent.[138] And the reasons given by Osama bin Laden for attacking the United States and Americans, both before and after 9/11, all referred to Middle Eastern affairs.[139] It was therefore natural that the concept of *global* terrorism became connected with the region of the Middle East. The connection between terrorism and the Middle East is not new: From the late 1960s, Palestinian hijackings and other activities such as the bombing of an American airliner over the Scottish town of Lockerbie in 1988, constituted the most significant expressions of *international* terrorism. Palestinian terrorist actions, particularly that carried out by the *Black September* group at the 1972 Munich Olympics, led to a greater political awareness of the Palestinian conflict. This was most significantly reflected in the famous 1974 speech made by PLO Chairman Yasser Arafat at the UN, and in the insistence of President Jimmy Carter on making the Palestinian conflict an important issue in the peace negotiations between Israel and Egypt which resulted in the 1978 Camp David Accords. Several steps were also taken towards greater international cooperation in the field of counter-terrorism, but this was largely limited to agreements concerning the tightening of airline security. Up until September 11, 2001, fighting terrorism largely remained a national concern for individual states, or the subject of bilateral cooperation such as that of France and Spain over the fight against the Basque separatist movement ETA.[140]

This situation changed dramatically after 9/11, and a characteristic new terminology emerged in which *global* terrorism replaced the older concept of international terrorism. At this time it also became common to refer to global terrorism as *new* terrorism, in an effort to emphasize that it was seen as different from that of previously known ethnic and political groups, from 19th-century anarchist activities to IRA, ETA, extreme left wing terrorism and ethnic separatism, and also as something new with regard to its use of transnational networks as a method of organization.[141]

The terms global and new terrorism, then, designate a phenomenon originating and rooted in a specific region, the Middle East, but also characterized by being universal. This is expressed in the way it is described by means of abstract concepts dislodged from historical, sociological and political contexts. The fact that it is universal depoliticizes the new terrorism, and instead turns it into a moral evil which threatens Western civilization's basic notions of freedom and tolerance.[142] What is new about the new terrorism, then, is not the fact that it springs from conflicts in the Middle East and between the West and Islamism, but rather that it represents a phenomenon and a threat which is predominantly interpreted in terms of moral, and often metaphysical, categories, rather than in political terms. Thus a 2005 State Department report describes the objectives of al-Qaida as apocalyptical and nihilistic, just as its formulaic descriptions equate all kinds of terrorist organizations and groups, ranging from al-Qaida to the Japanese Red Army.[143] It is made clear that the free world – as stated in the report – is faced with a formidable challenge posed by global terrorism, with global Jihad as the greatest danger. According to this view, terrorism is, on the one hand, a global and universal challenge and threat, belonging to no specific time or place, and, on the other hand, in its worst form related to the Middle East and Islam. This entails the following: that, as the background for and cause of the new terrorism, the political conflicts and problems which are associated with the Middle East are lifted into a universalistic, moral and metaphysical context; and that the fight against terrorism becomes a moral fight against evil rather than a struggle against a political enemy, who, motivated by religion and ideology and employing illegitimate means, revolts against the ruling international order in the Middle East. This turns the Islamic terrorist into 'the radical Other,' who, inhabiting a nihilistic and apocalyptic universe, can neither be understood nor reached, and must therefore be fought in a war fought beyond time and place.

Analyses of counter-terrorism strategies[144] before and after 9/11 clearly demonstrate that the attacks led to a transatlantic – in fact, global – acceptance of the American threat assessment developed during the Clinton administration, in which *new terrorism* was considered the primary and most immediate threat to global security after the Cold War.[145] Prior to 9/11, terrorism was not an issue on the European security policy agenda, which focused mainly on migration, particularly illegal immigration from Northern Africa and the Middle East. Terrorism was seen as either a matter for national concern or, with the establishment of the judicial cooperation after the Treaty of Maastricht, as one of a number of issues which were to be dealt with by the newly created Europol. But terrorism was not much of an issue, and the Europeans saw the American preoccupation with the threat as disproportionate, at times even hysterical, and certainly as a primarily American concern. The 9/11 attacks radically changed matters. The Europeans accepted the American threat assessment immediately and in its entirety, and from that point on, terrorism was considered a *global* problem.[146]

Paradoxically, this has not led to a greater understanding of the nature of terrorism, rather it has meant that the concept, now with the nomenclature *global* added to it, has become a collective designation, a metaphor, for all sorts of global and local threats such as the proliferation of weapons of mass destruction, the efforts of so-called 'rogue states' to develop such weapons, terrorist attacks such as those which the world has witnessed in Istanbul, Casablanca, Riyadh, Madrid and London, Palestinian suicide bombings, and the attacks on American occupation forces carried out by Iraqi resistance groups. The appreciation that the threat posed by the new terrorism is not solely directed at the United States, but constitutes a global threat, has, in terms of the political discourse, not led to a more accurate understanding of the nature of the new terrorism. On the contrary, a rather blurred and abstract notion regarding war on terror has emerged, which covers such diverse phenomena as war in Iraq, Israeli bombings of housing estates in Palestine, the tightening of legislation, and the development of an ambitious and costly preparedness against the threat of biological weapons. That the agreement to recognize terrorism as a global threat soon developed into a source of discord and outright conflict within the EU as well as across the Atlantic between Europe and the United States can be explained by the fact that the war on terror quickly came to encompass so much besides the actual fight against the Islamist networks allegedly responsible for the World Trade Center and Pentagon attacks.

The war in Iraq exemplifies this quite clearly. There were indeed many good reasons for removing Saddam Hussein. Yet very few outside of Washington were convinced that he had collaborated with the al-Qaida leader Osama bin Laden in the planning of the September 11 attacks, nor that they had systematically collaborated in any other way. It can certainly not be ruled out that groups affiliated with al-Qaida were on some level connected to groups within Iraq – but then the same is true of countries such as Lebanon, Syria, Iran, Yemen, and Saudi Arabia, as well as a number of countries in Asia and Africa.

The war in Iraq could have been explained from humanitarian motivations, as was the war in Kosovo. Instead, it was justified as a part of the war on terror. In this way, the war was instrumental in removing the focus from the fight against the Islamist networks, and some critics even claim that it effectively reinforced global terrorism. This is due in part to the narrow, American-led coalition war effort, not mandated by the UN, which increased the motivation for dissatisfied people in the Middle East and Asia to join the Islamic networks, and in part to the fact that resources and attention were almost exclusively turned towards Iraq – to some extent at the expense of the fight against militant Islamism.[147]

Certainly 9/11 directed enormous attention to the threat of global terrorism, which had previously been largely ignored by European countries, and which the Bush Administration had toned down in favor of a more state-oriented threat assessment. This new awareness, as well as a number of the initiatives it has generated, likely explain the fact that a number of terrorist plots in Europe and the United States have been uncovered and averted before proceeding to the 'smoking gun' stage.[148] This piece of good news does not, however, hide the fact that the war on terror fought on foreign soil emerges as a confused war on all fronts, with no clarity concerning *the identity of the enemy*. At home, it mainly takes the form of the building of domestic preparedness, though without a clear understanding of what exactly it is supposed to prepare us for or protect us against. As a case in point, many of the new EU initiatives merely refer to the abstractly defined concept of terrorism.[149]

New Terrorism
To the extent that its objective in fact *is* the elimination of terrorism, particularly of the Islamist networks responsible for 9/11, the abstract concept 'war on terror' can be broken down into more concretely defined phenomena. Some will object that it is impossible to draw up threat and risk assessments, because threats are by nature relative, and cannot be absolutely defined. Obviously, a threat cannot be absolutely and objectively identified, and the scope of a given threat cannot be precisely described by percentages. Threat assessments are indeed based

on interpretation, and the method of interpretation employed affects the way in which the threat may or will materialize: if the threat is ignored, it will by definition be greater than if it is addressed. On the other hand, preparedness is no guarantee that the threat will not materialize, and focusing on one type of threat may remove attention from others.

It does nonetheless seem to make good sense to concretize the rationale behind the various projects being launched with reference to the threat posed by global terrorism. It seems appropriate to break down the concept of 'war on terror' into a number of parts or sub-categories, which may then be individually considered in strategic and pragmatic terms, against a background of historical and societal analyses. In short, a re-contextualization of global terrorism within the historical contexts from which it springs will serve to de-mystify it, and place it in a more pragmatic and realistic perspective. In overall terms, it can be useful to distinguish between threats posed by terrorism, threats posed by states such as North Korea, and the threat posed by the proliferation of weapons of mass destruction. Within the category of terrorism, it may then be useful to distinguish between global and local terrorism, the latter meaning terrorism which is clearly related to local or regional conflicts, such as those in Northern Ireland, the Basque Country and Palestine.

Global or new terrorism refers to terrorist organizations which see the whole world as a potential battlefield. This means that they are branched out globally, and that they specifically and credibly threaten to carry out attacks anywhere on the globe. So far only one such global organization has emerged: al-Qaida. The fact that al-Qaida was globally based, however, did not entail that the geographical perspective of the organization was global: as made clear in countless publications issued by Osama bin Laden and other al-Qaida members, such as Ayman al-Zawahiri, their objective was not world domination, it was specifically to rid Islamic territory of foreign occupiers. This means freeing territory, for centuries mainly occupied by Muslims, from occupation by non-Muslims: for instance freeing Palestine from Israeli-Jewish occupation; Chechnya from Russian-Christian occupation; Saudi Arabia and the remaining Gulf states, including Iraq, from American-Christian occupation; Kashmir from Indian-Hindu occupation, and the Mindanao Peninsula from Filipino-Christian occupation.[150] The liberation of

Afghanistan in the 1980s from Russian-Christian occupation serves as the glorious example to be followed.

The novelty of global terrorism, then, is not that it is unrelated to specific political conflicts.

Rather, the novelty consists in a number of other aspects: Firstly, its *field of operation* is not limited to specific countries or areas. In principle, it directs its attacks against its enemies wherever in the world they might reside. It is thus credible that Islamist networks have been and are involved in terrorism and attempts at terrorism in the Caucasus, Central Asia, South East Asia, South Asia, Africa, Europe, and the United States. Everywhere they take advantage of local conflicts in their revolutionary revolt against what they see as Western and American domination and occupation of Islamic territory. This leads to the second aspect: that the objective or goal of al-Qaida terrorism is an omnipotent desire to free this territory with a view to reinstating the Caliphate, that is, to reestablish the Islamic empire which finally collapsed with the 1924 dissolution of the Ottoman Empire after the First World War – an event referred to by al-Qaida as 'the disaster.' As abstract as this objective may be, it does however appeal widely to individuals living in relatively isolated and marginalized pockets of the global village, whether in American metropolises or rural areas of Pakistan. The image emerging of today's Islamist is reminiscent of that of the militant Communist of the past.

Thirdly, al-Qaida must at the present point be understood as an ideology, or as a metaphor for a widely spread-out network of individuals who rarely have anything in common in concrete terms other than abstract ideology, the will to fight, and a fundamentalist conviction that they are participating in a meaningful, global battle over values.

Up until the American war in Afghanistan in the fall of 2001, al-Qaida was a well-organized network, with headquarters and training facilities in the Afghan mountains. After the war, however, it has been transformed into a loose network which operates locally, often without any real contact with the established al-Qaida leadership. There are clear signs that the 9/11 attacks and the subsequent war on terror, particularly the wars in Afghanistan and Iraq, have lead to an increase in support for the ideology and the projects of al-Qaida within many Muslim communities. The war on terror has thus had a dual effect on al-Qaida: on the one hand, it has lead to a marked weakening of the original organization, including an impairment of its ability to carry out large-scale and spectacular attacks like that of September 11, 2001. On the other hand, it has disseminated the ideology, and thereby in effect expanded the recruitment base for the Islamist networks. This seems to have at once reduced the risk of attacks on buildings and institutions of great symbolic value, such as the New York World Trade Center attack, but also increased the risk of attacks on other targets, such as the Madrid train station in 2004 or the London subway in 2005. This dissemination of the ideology of al-Qaida cannot be explained and understood if the ideology is interpreted exclusively in moral and metaphysical terms. It must be seen in relation to the historical and political contexts referred to in its construal of itself. As convincingly demonstrated by former CIA analyst Michael Scheur[151] in his much commended book *Through Our Enemy's Eyes,* al-Qaida and Osama bin Laden do not base their *Jihad* on a hatred of Western and American liberal values, but on a hatred of and revolt against the policy led by the West and the United States in the Middle East. Or, as Scheur puts it: the Islamists do not hate us because of our freedoms and our values, but because of what we politically have done and are doing in the Middle East, as well as in other Muslim societies.[152]

The Ideology of Al-Qaida
The history of al-Qaida goes back to the Afghan Mujahedin resistance against the Soviet occupation of Afghanistan, which lasted from December 1979 until the withdrawal in 1989. With American, Saudi and Pakistani backing, the Afghan Mujahedin received weapons, funds and training in support of the resistance. Throughout the war, there was a steady influx of Muslim volunteers from Central Asia, South and South East Asia, as well as the Middle East and Africa, who wanted to take part in the struggle against the Soviet occupation. The objective was to rid Islamic soil of the infidel Russians. Recruitment and training was organized out of an office in the Pakistani-Afghan border town of Peshawar. It was carried out under the leadership of the Jordanian Palestinian Abdullah Azzam, together with, among others, Osama bin Laden, who later in the war established an actual Arab brigade of volunteers from the Arab Middle East and North Africa. Later in the 1980s, this became the recruitment base for al-Qaida, which was, however, also joined by people

The Globalization of Al-Qaida's Battle over Values 133

Having been an exporter of Jihad to Afghanistan in the 1980s, in the 1990s Saudi Arabia itself became a target of al-Qaida terrorism. Yet only after major attacks on residential areas in 2004 did the Saudi government launch a hunt for Jihadists within its own territory.

from South East Asia, Africa, and Central Asia. The exact date of the founding of al-Qaida is uncertain, 1988 or 1989, but this is likely due to the fact that the organization was the result of a process spanning several months, not of a founding proper. 'Al-Qaida,' which in Arabic means 'the base', started out as a mere designation for the place(s) in which Osama bin Laden resided. Later, when a comprehensive reorganization took place in Afghanistan, it naturally came to designate the organization as a whole. Initially, al-Qaida was supposed to serve as a kind of emergency unit which, as had been the case in Afghanistan, was able to intervene on the side of Muslims fighting occupation forces elsewhere, such as in Central Asia and Kashmir.[153] Under the inspiration of former leaders of the Egyptian Jihadists, the purpose of al-Qaida was later defined as the liberation of Arab countries from heretical Arab regimes, with a particular focus on Algeria, Egypt, and Saudi Arabia.[154]

Al-Qaida's main objective changed once more with the establishment of American military bases in the Arab states in the Gulf in 1991, in connection with the war against Iraq, and the goal now became to eject the United States from the Middle East. This project enjoyed great popularity among Arab populations, and continues to do so.[155] The reasons for this were, firstly, that it is common in the Middle East to perceive the American military presence in the Arab Gulf as a de facto occupation, meant to ensure American domination over the vast Arab oil reserves. Secondly, it was widely believed that the United States was in the business of bolstering Arab regimes considered illegitimate by the Islamists. This belief was nourished by the close cooperation between the United States and the Saudi royal family as well as the Emir families of the Gulf states, in addition to the considerable U.S. economic support for Egypt. Thirdly, the United States' substantial economic and military support for Israel is seen as a necessary condition for the maintenance of the Israeli, Jewish occupation of Islamic Palestine.[156] For the Middle East to be liberated and Islam to be reinstated as the form of government in a reestablishment of the Islamic empire, which in its heyday extended from the South of Spain, through North Africa and the Middle East, and into the Balkans, it was, according to al-Qaida, absolutely necessary that the Americans be ejected from the Middle East. The presence of the United States and its allies in the Middle East, and their support for Israel, is likened by al-Qaida to the medieval Christian crusades sponsored by the Roman Catholic Church. This view is substantiated with careful reference to famous battles in which Muslims defended themselves against the Crusaders' Holy War against Islam.[157] The Jihad waged by al-Qaida against the United States and the West is thus interpreted as a defense against the infidels' incursion into, and ravage and plunder of, the House of Islam *(Dar al-Islam)*. *Jihad* is nowhere interpreted as a strategy for the conquest of non-Muslim or Western territory; neither in the official ideology of Osama bin Laden, nor in that of al-Qaida, as expressed in countless publications, interviews and speeches, including those distributed to Western media via video and cassette tapes.[158] Rather, it is understood as a defense against Western and American aggression in the Islamic world. This construal of Jihad as defense is derived from classical Islamic texts, and it is with reference to these that terrorism against Western, Jewish and American target is legitimized.[159]

The formulation in the famous 1998 declaration *Jihad Against Jews and Crusaders,* that it is the duty of every Muslim to kill Americans wherever they may be,[160] is derived from a particular interpretation of a religious imperative; it now obliges Muslims to defend Islamic territory against that which is seen as American aggression. It does not express an ambition to conquer either the West or America.

In the eyes of Osama bin Laden and his fellow ideologists, the interpretation of the Jihad in the form of terrorism, mainly against U.S. targets, as a religiously and politically justified *defensive war* legitimizes certain deeds otherwise banned under Islam, except when the House of Islam is under siege. Al-Qaida thus brings together two types of argument in a synthesis legitimizing terrorist actions such as 9/11 and a number of other things, such as the fact that the great majority of the victims of the 1998 terrorist actions in East Africa were Muslims, or the necessity of cooperating with infidels in the planning and carrying out of terrorist attacks. Osama bin Laden has specifically addressed these matters by arguing that, as far the killing of Muslims in al-Qaida terrorist attacks is concerned, the loss of a few hundred lives is but a necessary price in the war against the aggressor, the United States, which is responsible for the murder of half a million children through the imposition of sanctions on Iraq. As for the second, Islam allows the faithful to cooperate with infidels if it serves a higher cause such as the defense of Islamic territory.[161] The bin Laden interpretation of Islamic tradition, then, offers no objection to a cooperative effort between Saddam Hussein and al-Qaida in the latter's Jihad against the United States. That this did not occur must be ascribed to other, most likely practical and political, factors. The religious line of argument interprets the situation in the Middle East as an expression of dominance and aggression by a United States out to conquer and occupy Islamic land. This interpretation is substantiated by and ties into the political line of argumentation, which interprets the U.S. military presence in the Arabian Gulf and her support for the illegitimate Arab regimes as a ploy to ensure cheap oil supplies.

According to Osama bin Laden, U.S. support for Israel serves the same purpose; the oppression of Muslims and the exploitation of Arab resources. According to the religious rationale, the U.S. presence in the Middle East, then, is thought to be a modern Christian crusade against Islam, which it, according to Islamic tradition, is the duty of every Muslim to strive against. The parallel argument in the realm of politics is that the American presence in the Middle East is an expression of classic imperialism. Both arguments have consistently been present in al-Qaida publications and declarations, and are widely accepted in Muslim as well as non-Muslim anti-Imperialist circles around the world. On the basis of speeches by Osama bin Laden and tracts published by Ayman al-Zawahiri,[162] we may conclude that the al-Qaida ideology is neither nihilist nor apocalyptic, but boils down to a fundamentalist, religiously motivated anti-imperialist rejection of the implementation of the Middle East policies of the U.S. and the West, since the dissolution of the Ottoman Empire at the hands of the Western powers after the First World War. However, in his speeches Osama bin Laden often makes reference to eschatological and apocalyptical visions. For instance in the speech addressing the Muhammad drawings, which was published on April 26, 2006, by *as-Sahab*, in which bin Laden refers to the state of tribulation in which we live, the final days before the Day of Judgment. Most of the speech, though, is concerned with rendering the political conflicts of the day.

The ideology of al-Qaida is rooted in the Saudi Wahhabist movement and in Egyptian Islamic fundamentalism. At the same time, al-Qaida puts forth a clearly formulated anti-imperialist critique of the United States which closely resembles the traditional arguments of Arab nationalist and socialist groups. Consequently, the pan-Islamic nationalism of al-Qaida has a broad appeal, resonating with those in the Arab world who stand in opposition to their governments and who have lost faith in U.S. policy towards the Middle East. However, the widespread sympathy, and probable support, among Arab populations for al-Qaida's ideology and criticism does not necessarily entail support for al-Qaida's strategies and use of terrorism. The French political scientist and Islam scholar Gilles Kepel has convincingly argued that the al-Qaida strategy has in fact failed.[163] This strategy, as formulated by the Egyptian al-Qaida leader al-Zawahri in a pamphlet subsequently published in the Egyptian newspaper *al-sharg al-awsat*, may be understood as a variant of the Leninist theory of the vanguard: al-Qaida's acts of terror are supposed to cause the Muslim masses to rise up against the Arab governments and their Western allies.[164] So far this has not come to pass.

The ideology nevertheless seems to be spreading, in the Middle East as well as elsewhere. The only explanation for this is that many Muslims agree that the issues raised by al-Qaida are vital, and have become even more important as hopes for a resolution of the Israel-Palestine conflict have waned and the U.S. lacks the will to force through a solution. The war in Iraq has also hardened the stance of many Muslims against the United States and the West. Post-war developments in Iraq have revealed a considerable convergence between a secular nationalist opposition and an Islamist, al-Qaida inspired criticism of the United States and the West.

The continuation of the war on terror through the war in Iraq, without a UN mandate or broad international or Arab support; U.S. support for the brutal suppression of the opposition by Arab governments in the name of counter-terrorism; the suspension of international law at Guantanamo; and the Abu Ghraib prisoner torture scandal, have all contributed to a greater receptivity to Islamist criticism of the United States among Muslims. Faith in the ability of the political establishment in Washington to solve the political problems of Arabs and Muslims has plummeted as a result of the war.

Gilles Kepel is no doubt correct in claiming that the al-Qaida strategy in connection with the September 11 attacks has proved wrong for the simple reason that the great majority of Muslims in and outside the Middle East do not recognize or believe in terrorism as a means to solving current political problems; however, al-Qaida has indeed succeeded in the dissemination of its ideology, which is probably due to its political thematization of certain basic problems in the relations between the Middle East and the West, within a framework of understanding which is recognized by many Muslims. Some Western Muslim subscribers to this framework of understanding find justification for these views in the immigration policies of their respective countries of residence.

Using the Media

Al-Qaida has craftily taken advantage of the enormous media focus on Osama bin Laden and the Islamist networks in the aftermath of 9/11, as a means of spreading their message. Statements made by Osama bin Laden and al-Qaida spokesmen were instantly broadcast to the world by *al-Jazeera, al-Arabia*, CNtN, BBC World and other satellite networks. Bin Laden responded promptly to the U.S. invasion of Afghanistan by issuing a statement to the effect that al-Qaida's struggle constituted a reaction to the infidel occupation of Islamic lands, specifically Palestine. Al-Qaida leaders or groups claiming to represent al-Qaida have also produced statements and demands in connection with later events. One example of the latter is that of the *Abu Hafs al-Misri Brigades*, an unknown group whose first appearance in cyberspace was a statement which denied Sunni al-Qaida-related involvement in the major bombing in Kerbala, Iraq, on March 2, 2004, which killed more than 100 Shias. About a week later, the group assumed responsibility for the March 11 Madrid bombings with the following statement: " …death squads have reached the heart of the Europe of the Crusaders, striking a painful blow against one of the crusading nations (Spain) … This is but one small sum in the reckoning with the crusading nation of Spain, an ally of the United States in the war against Islam … We of the *Abu Hafs al-Misri Brigades* are unconcerned by so-called 'civilian' losses … Are they allowed to kill our children, our wives, our young and our old in Afghanistan, Iraq, Pakistan, and Kashmir? Are we then not allowed to kill them?" The name of the group refers to the Egyptian Mohammed Atef, also known as Abu Hafs, who was the military leader of al-Qaida until his death during the American bombings of Afghanistan in November 2001. The Madrid bombings, which took place only days before a parliamentary election, helped bring to power a new government, which in turn brought about the withdrawal of Spanish troops from Iraq. Whether or not this was a genuine al-Qaida statement, radicalized Islamists take full advantage of the terrorist attack in issuing political statements on the situation in Iraq, and on what they see as the United States' crusade against the House of Islam. In this way they are able to communicate threats against the coalition in Iraq as well as to spread the ideology of a religious war to what al-Zawahiri calls the Islamic Nation, or the Muslim masses. Islamist groups in Iraq – some of which probably only exist in cyberspace – are equally proficient and morbidly cynical in their use of the media.[165] The September 11 attacks have thus allowed al-Qaida to carve out a place for themselves with the international media, from which position they can issue threats and communicate their ideology to the entire world.

The Glocal Organization of Terrorism

Studies of al-Qaida-related terrorist acts in New York in 1993, in East Africa in 1998, and of course September 11, 2001, reveal the same pattern: individuals trained in terrorism established contact with isolated communities of likeminded Islamists in need of training. After establishing contact these terrorist mentors helped organize terrorist actions.

In other words, competent and well-trained outsiders were sent to launch and carry out one or more terrorist actions through the creation of local ad-hoc groups, as seen in Turkey in November 2003. After the act the group would cease to exist, for which reason the term 'group' in its classic sense is only really applicable to these ad-hoc organizations by observers of a bureaucratic, categorizing mindset. It is more appropriate to think of these terrorist cells as temporary links between global and local networks; the term *glocal* springs to mind. The connection between trained Jihadists and local operators was established by a scout, responsible for recruiting local talent within the communities.

This *glocal* terrorism can of course only to a limited extent be fought by military means. There is little doubt that the destruction of al-Qaida training facilities and strongholds in Afghanistan by the actions of the U.S. military in October 2001 greatly weakened the network. But this also served to spread the al-Qaida network to many other countries, where new strongholds were established in regions beyond government control.

Islamist networks subsist on money, people, and conflict. Counterterrorism measures must therefore address these three areas. Terrorism has traditionally been financed by a combination of financial crime, drug trafficking, hostage taking, robberies, and piracy, as well as fundraisings, donations, and legitimate business activities. Money is transferred without the use of banks, by means of the *hawala* system and couriers. After 9/11 much has been done to limit this money flow, especially with the November 2001 UN convention. In addition, a number of countries have tightened legislation on this issue. Saudi Arabia, which is thought to have been one of the most significant sources of finance for Islamist networks, is a recent addition to this group. Research done by the UN, American think tanks, and U.S. congressional committees, shows that the results are somewhat meager for the simple reason that it is extraordinarily difficult to follow and stem flows of money.[166] Experts expect little gain from further measures in this area. Such measures would in any case be a major impediment to legitimate international business.[167]

Experience shows that Islamist networks reside in three main areas: Firstly, the weak states in the Middle East, South Asia, South East Asia, and Africa provide Islamist networks with the opportunity to establish themselves literally beyond the law. In these areas, the only way to fight the dissemination of Islamist networks is to strengthen the infrastructure and territorial integrity of the states, to improve their national police forces, intelligence services, and court systems, and work with them in carrying out investigations, making arrests – possibly including the military suppression of any terrorist camps which may be discovered – and conduct trials. It is critically important that these initiatives take the form of constructive collaboration between the wealthy donor countries and these weak states. The EU-Mediterranean partnership known as the Barcelona Process might serve as the model. In other words, the key terms in the construction of a common security response are dialogue, cooperation, and development.

Secondly, many members of Islamist networks turn out to have been recruited from communities and mosques in Western cities such as London, Hamburg, Paris, and Madrid, or, as in the cases of Istanbul and Casablanca, from small communities in which the al-Qaida ideology was already widespread. Here, sympathizers ready to move on to the next level of militant activism were comparatively easily found. That did not mean that these communities organized terrorism; rather, contact between global and local networks could be established here through the recruitment of sympathizers. London has long harbored communities whose ideology and rhetoric closely resemble those of al-Qaida. British authorities have likely been aware that individuals recruited from the Finsbury Park Mosque milieu received training in Pakistan and Afghanistan and subsequently fought in conflicts around the world, notably in the Caucasus.[168] Similar milieus have existed elsewhere in Europe, and national authorities have generally more or less chosen to ignore these as long as they were not actively planning terrorist attacks to be carried out within the respective countries. The partial planning and organization of the September 11 attacks in Hamburg is an illustration of the fact that Europe has served as a staging ground for terrorist networks looking, for instance, to acquire passports and other necessities. After

September 11 European countries recognized that their traditional and pragmatic laissez faire approach is not a tenable response to glocal terrorism. National authorities in the United Kingdom, Germany, Belgium, France, and Italy and Spain have therefore after the 2004 Madrid bombings chosen to prioritize surveillance of the communities in question. A similar effort has been made to strengthen national intelligence services as well as the international cooperation between services.

A purposive intelligence effort is necessary if terrorist attacks on European soil are to be prevented. But efficient intelligence work entails more than electronic intelligence gathering, police searches and raids; contacts must be established within the communities where the local and the global networks meet.[169] A crucial step is the prevention of ghettoization. Terrorist acts in Morocco, Kenya, Indonesia, and Turkey have been organized in such self-regulating, isolated communities as ghettos are known to present. Ramzi Yusef recruited and organized his project group for the 1993 attack on the World Trade Center from such an isolated community in New Jersey.[170] Secondly, maintaining good relations with immigrant and minority communities is useful in the gathering of information on potential terrorist-related activities, as people in these communities generally abhor terrorism as much as the rest of society. Such dialogue is also important with a view to preventing the radicalization of such communities which may result from social marginalization.[171]

Conflict between society and whole ethnic immigrant groups will certainly not be conducive for the prevention and combating of terrorism. Quite to the contrary, as the French Islam scholar Olivier Roy has argued, integration, dialogue and intelligence work combined present the best path ahead.

Islamic Networks in Zones of Conflict

The third field of operations for Islamist networks is constituted by zones of conflict in which Muslims are involved; examples include Bosnia in the 1990s, Chechnya, Kashmir, Algeria, Pakistan, Afghanistan, and, most recently, Iraq. Such conflicts may be considered al-Qaida's raison d'etre: On the one hand these conflicts constitute and are exploited by the network as motivating factors, while, on the other hand, they serve to provide a logical culmination to the individual Jihadist's recruitment, training, and deployment. Particularly before the events of 9/11 led to the implementation of much stricter surveillance measures on the Internet, accounts of Islamist or Jihadist activity were prominent on Islamist websites. In other words, wars and conflicts motivate Islamist sympathizers to join the struggle. The manner in which these conflicts are dealt with by the opponents of the Islamists, the West, is therefore of critical importance. It would certainly be preferable if the conflicts were simply resolved, but obviously this is not immediately realistic. The alternative is that conflicts are handled with great *legitimacy*, that is, with widespread international support, including the support of the parties involved in the region, and, furthermore, they must be handled without serious violations of international law such as torture, secret internments, and excessive use of military force leading to great civilian losses.[172]

From this perspective, the difference between the wars in Afghanistan and Iraq is striking. The first war saw broad support for the U.S. intervention among the UN, NATO, the European Union, the Arab countries, the neighboring countries in Central Asia, and, not least, from Russia, Pakistan, and India. The U.S. response was seen as justified in the light of 9/11. Widespread popular opposition to the war did manifest, however, especially in the region itself, where the opposition to Pakistani President Pervez Musharraf's support for the United States was cause for some concern. Wide international support and foreign aid to Pakistan have so far helped to avoid increased instability in the country. An additional joint effort by the United States and Russia to contain the Kashmir conflict, following great tension between regional nuclear powers India and Pakistan, has succeeded to the point where a thaw in the relations between these arch enemies seems credible.[173] The war in Iraq, on the other hand, enjoyed meager international and regional support. As a result, controlling the conflicts in Iraq as well as in nearby Pakistan has become a very difficult task. It is rumored that former employees of the Pakistani nuclear weapons program have contacted Islamist networks presumably interested in acquiring weapons of mass destruction.[174] The possibility that the dissemination of nuclear technology to weak states has become more likely as a result of the war in Iraq, as proposed by the former Director of the CIA, George Tenet, in his 2003 annual report to Congress concerning global threats, can thus not be ruled out.[175]

The reality of the situation, then, may well be that the reduction of threats from so-called rogue states under some circumstances leads to a strengthening of Islamist networks and consequently to an increased threat of terrorism, including terrorist attacks involving weapons of mass destruction.

It is impossible to determine whether the existence of a broad coalition behind the war in Iraq would have changed this paradox, but it seems self-evident that support from countries in and outside the region would provided better opportunities for handling the situation in Iraq, as well as other conflicts in the region.

Jihad on the Internet: Local Networks

International relations of today are obviously characterized by controversy and conflict. Still, what we defined in the introductory chapter as the Islamist community of interpretation increasingly manifests itself as opposition to the liberal-humanist order which the Western democracies are attempting to disseminate globally. Iraq and the Middle East continue to serve as the laboratory for such Western experimentation. Though states such as Iran and Saudi Arabia are clearly advocating an Islam-based political order, it is noteworthy that the Islamist community of interpretation is transnational to a much greater extent than the liberal-humanist community of interpretation, which, particularly in the West, is mostly rooted in the state. This may be explained by noting that Islamists in virtually every country are prohibited from participating in government-level politics. Once more Iran presents the exception, as does Saudi Arabia to a certain extent. The Saudi strategy of legitimization rests on government control of Islamism through Islamic councils and imams. This has not prevented a significant Islamist opposition from manifesting itself within the kingdom as well as in exile, notably in London. Islamists have achieved some level of representation within the political systems of Jordan and Egypt. Their presence is, however, suffered only to the extent that the respective governments are able to control them. This fans the flames of Islamist criticism and anger. Islamists see the Arab regimes, including the Saudi royal family, as corrupt and deviant regimes which keep the opposition from power with the assistance of Western countries – except in those places where the West has forced through elections.

As mentioned above it would be wrong to think of the Islamist opposition as a homogenous group. It would be even more wrong to think that all Islamists embrace the use of violence and terrorism in their struggle against the reigning order. That is not the case. Nevertheless, Islamists who distance themselves from terrorism agree with militant Islamist networks which embrace violent Jihad as far as the criticism of Western foreign policy and Western domestically implemented national security measures are concerned. In Western terminology, the Islamist community of interpretation can roughly be divided into two main camps: Jihadists and Islamists, of which the latter reject the use of terrorism. While the Islamists reject terrorism and violence as a political means, they frequently employ Jihadist rhetoric, which tends to blur the distinction.

What may give rise to concerns is that the Jihadist camp is apparently expanding, not only in Iraq, Saudi Arabia, and Yemen, but within European countries. In other words it seems that as the war on terror, in the broadest sense of the term, escalates, a radicalization is taking place among Islamists in European countries. It is even more worrying that the radicalization in Europe seems to be taking place independently of any outside influence. There are still no indications that the Jihadists behind the Madrid bombings on March 11, 2004, which killed 198 people, had received any outside support or had been in physical contact with international Islamists familiar with the practicalities of planning terrorist attacks. Similarly, no evidence has emerged that the four men who blew themselves up in London on July 7, 2005 had received any outside support. Some point to the fact that at least three, and possibly all four, of the suicide bombers had spent time in Pakistan, presumably receiving ideological and possibly terrorist training. Yet there are no indications that they had been recruited and sent to Pakistan, rather than going on their own initiative. It is often argued that visiting Islamist imams from Saudi Arabia, Pakistan, Egypt, and Lebanon are, through their Friday prayers and study groups, indirectly responsible for the radicalization of young men belonging to European immigrant communities. It is all the more remarkable, then, that the Leeds mosque attended by the London suicide bombers was in fact highly critical of their growing radicalization, to the point where the bombers chose to meet instead in an abandoned store. All available evidence indicates that the terrorist cells in London and Madrid were local through and through. Judging from the individual profiles of the bombers, no particularly clear-cut image emerges: several of them were educated and held down jobs, while others were regular dropouts with some sort of criminal record.[176] Why and how they got together and decided to plan and carry out major terrorist actions is a question we may never be able to answer. The answer to the question of how they managed to carry out the attacks is more easily answered: the Internet.

The Retirement of the Talent Scout?

As early as the 1990s it was well known that the Internet played a vital role in the organization of the al-Qaida network. The Internet was used to spread the Islamist message, for propaganda purposes, and for the recruitment of Jihadists for the training camps in Afghanistan. At the completion of their training they would go to Bosnia, Chechnya, Kashmir, the Philippines, Algeria, Egypt, Saudi Arabia, or be singled out for special assignments such as the 1998 Embassy bombings in East Africa and the attacks on New York and Washington on September 11, 2001. The notorious website azzam.com, named after Abdullah Azzam, the co-founder of al-Qaida, was shut down after 9/11, but while in existence had done much for the recruitment of Jihadists with, for instance, its online catalogue of battle sequences filmed in Chechnya and other places. Al-Qaida switched to different means of communication, such as Hotmail and chatrooms, after a CIA leak had alerted bin Laden to the fact that U.S. intelligence was wiretapping his satellite phone. But though it was well known at the time that for instance instructions for the construction of bombs were available on the Internet, the Internet apparently did not play any significant role in the operational planning of terrorist actions. Instead, couriers and regular training in Afghanistan were key, and large-scale operations were directed by high-ranking members of al-Qaida. Though the network took full advantage of the blessings of globalization and the information society, al-Qaida of that period was a hierarchical organization whose leaders created and directed individual cells, whose assignments, although carried out independently, were handed down and approved by the leadership, which also provided logistical and other support. The objective was clear: to direct attacks at America with a view to forcing the superpower out of the Middle East, and incite the

Arab masses to rise up against the illegitimate Arab governments. Their crowning achievement was September 11, which, it seems, was also the last real al-Qaida action, given that the United States' war in Afghanistan destroyed the organization and its training facilities. The leaders were killed, caught, or forced to flee. Among them were Osama bin Laden and Ayman al-Zawahiri, who are now believed to reside in the border regions of Pakistan and Afghanistan, deprived of operational options other than the issuing of speeches and threats, which are for example broadcast by the Arab satellite television network *al-Jazeera*.

If the main objective of the U.S. war in Afghanistan was to destroy the al-Qaida organization, the war was an unqualified success. If, however, the objective was to combat and prevent terrorism, it has fallen far short of the goal. The former heads of the U.S. National Security Council Daniel Benjamin and Steven Simon have pointed out that three-fourths of the suicide terrorist actions registered by the RAND Corporation think tank since the introduction of this (suicide bombing) strategy by the Tamil Tigers in 1968, have been carried out after September 11, 2001. The large-scale terrorist attacks on Bali, in Casablanca, Istanbul, Riyadh, Madrid, Beslan, London, and Sharm al-Shaikh, the range of lesser terrorist actions carried out by Islamists in various areas of the world, and the attacks that have been averted in Europe, are all indications that Islamist terrorists are extremely active. Although the number of victims is small compared to the numbers killed in the war on terror in Afghanistan and Iraq, the fact remains that the frequency of terrorist acts carried out by pan-Islamist networks has increased dramatically since 9/11.

The vast majority of these acts were apparently organized by local networks without the support of so-called Afghanistan veterans, who received their training fighting the Soviet occupation of Afghanistan in the 1980s and constituted the backbone of the al-Qaida organization until 9/11. The strategy of the time was that veterans of the war in Afghanistan recruited locally and formed project groups. This lead to the theory of the talent scout who was sent into specific areas in order to recruit locals for local actions. There are many indications that this type of recruitment process lost significance with the defeat of the established al-Qaida organization in 2001. The terrorist networks of today are established locally by small groups of radicalized Islamists, for instance in Muslim immigrant communities in European societies. This tendency does not rule out the possibility that ad-hoc groups may still be formed by talent scouts, just as local groups in different European countries may well cooperate with like-minded groups in other countries via the Internet or by other means.

Globalized Islam: A Political Community

Olivier Roy has suggested the term 'globalized Islam' for a new type of Islamist radicalization which in his opinion is growing fast among young immigrants in Europe. 'Globalized' is meant to convey that these second and third generation Muslim immigrants are highly critical of the European societies in which they live, yet at the same time they reject their countries of origin including their dominant culture and Islamic tradition. In a short article, "Euroislam: The Jihad within", Roy distinguishes between a type of radicalization that is of a mainly nationalist nature, referring to for instance the Palestinian and Kurdish struggles for national and political independence, and a different type of radicalization which is oriented towards an abstract and imagined global Islamic community. Roy notes that "the second form of radicalization is ideological and is expressed as a supranational Islam not related to the country of origin." He goes on: "the Islamic radicalization in Europe since the early 1990s has mainly been of this second kind, oriented towards a supranational community, the Muslim *umma*. This community is to some extent an imaginary construct, but is experienced as real. This state of affairs is consolidated by the Islamic subculture on the Internet."[177]

Roy has mainly focused on the influx of young Muslims into the political environments surrounding mosques in major European cities. However, new research on Islamist websites indicates that the meeting place for the new kind of Jihadists is on the Internet. Since 9/11, the Internet has undergone a revolution in terms of sophistication, the choice of products on offer, and content. Institutes such as the SITE Institute and the Intel Center; consulting businesses such as the Washington-based DFI International which does contract work for the U.S. government; and last but not least analysts at the Norwegian Defense Research Institute (FFI), monitor and analyze developments on Islamist websites. These experts have established that the Internet currently provides all the information and instruction a local group needs in order to carry out a terrorist attack. Benjamin and Simon aptly summarize many salient points in *The Next Attack*, while Brynjar Lia has presented the results of extensive studies of *"jihad online"* in the article "Al-Qaeda Online: Understanding Jihadist Infrastructure" (*Jane's Intelligence Review*, January 2006).[178] As was the case in the 1990s, the Internet of today is used for the purposes of communicating messages, propaganda, and for purposes of recruitment, though now with considerably greater technical skill. In the 1990s violent video clips from Chechnya were meant to motivate potential Jihadists, whereas today decapitation scenes from Iraq are getting an enormous amount of attention. Benjamin and Simon point out that these videos are downloaded by the millions. The May 2004 decapitation of American telecommunications entrepreneur Nicholas Berg is particularly popular. One website noted a record download rate of 15 million. Though many people besides Islamists may find the viewing of these brutal images interesting (or sexually arousing), there can be little doubt that Jihadists are using them to convey the message that they are strong and determined in their resistance to the American superpower.

Jihad Online

There are however at least three new developments which, on the one hand, support and complement Roy's observations of a mounting radicalization in the construction of a globalized Islamism and what we have defined as pan-Islamic nationalism; on the other hand, these developments add to our understanding of how small, physically isolated groups such as the one behind the London subway bombings are able to plan terrorist attacks, including the construction of bombs.

The meeting places on the Internet provide a sense of belonging to a global community. These websites provide their users with the opportunity to identify with a close-up, virtual society, as an alternative to identifying with the society in which the individual user lives or the society he or his parents emigrated from. This in itself contributes to the creation of a global *umma*. Ethnicity, national identity and traditional religious and cultural hierarchies lose their influence to a globalized Islamism which makes no distinction between the struggles of Muslims in, say, Gaza or the Northern Caucasus: they are all equally urgent and important, or equally remote and vague. They serve mainly as points of reference and as arguments to be employed in the concretization of a world view in which Muslims are at war with Jews and Christian Crusaders. National and cultural differences are of no consequence here and are lost; so too the aura of importance enjoyed by traditional authorities. Some observers hold that the radicalization of Islamic scholars is to a large degree due to the threat to their authority posed by the horizontal structure of the Internet, which allows anyone with a computer to contribute their interpretations of religious dogma. In a manner similar to that in which the printing press provided the European Renaissance with a mass media which over the centuries contributed to the development of a written culture which proved increasingly difficult for governments to control, the Internet and satellite television negate governmental attempts to control the flow of information. This does not necessarily entail increased support for critical, secular, and Enlightenment values; rather, as was the case with the invention of the printing press, the new media are used to criticize those very values.[179] The battle for the Muslim mind takes place on satellite television and on the Internet, where Islamic scholars with access to the media, such as the Qatar-based Sheikh Qaradawi on *al-Jazeera*, spread their Islamist messages on a variety of topics, including the Muhammad drawings. One may assume that Qaradawi had to take part in that particular debate in order to retain his prominent status in Muslim communities in the Middle East and in Europe. His hostile stance towards *Jyllands-Posten*'s drawings and Denmark may in fact be an expression of his own views. Yet it is equally possible that he assumed that particular position because he is competing with radical Islamists for the attention of the Islamists. Satellite television as well as the Internet are creating a public sphere in which everyone may speak their mind, but there is no guarantee that this mass media culture in itself will lead to democratization and public support for Western values such as freedom of speech. The end result may just as easily be an increase in Islamism and fundamentalism.

The Internet of today offers instant answers to all sorts of questions, including more technical ones. One may, for instance, obtain professional assistance in connection with the handling of chemicals when making bombs. These discussions take place in private, password-protected fora. Here, questions concerning the manifold bomb-making manuals available on the Internet can be asked and answered. Another interesting observation is that strategic and political discussions, analyses, and commentaries are increasingly prevalent on Islamist websites. Norwegian scholars Brynjar Lia and Thomas Hegghammer thus came across documents detailing how to organize efficiently the Islamist resistance in Iraq. These analyses revealed great insight into American strategic thought and theories of security policy. Strategies for the Iraqi resistance and strategies for undermining the coherency of the coalition were discussed using candid, largely non-religious terminology. It was argued that the United States would recall her forces if the economic burden of building a democratic Iraq grew too heavy. Consequently, the strategic paper called for the sabotage of building projects, oil facilities, and of the coherency of the coalition, through a war of attrition which would eventually place the entire burden of the war on the United States. A detailed study indicated that Spain constituted the weakest link in the coalition, and that an attack on Spanish interests before the general election would topple the Conservative government. The new government would withdraw the Spanish troops from Iraq. This would set off a chain reaction of withdrawals by other countries. Hegghammer and Lia are not able to document that the Jihadists responsible for the Madrid bombings had knowledge of this analysis, but it is noteworthy that the Jihadist online discourse is increasingly dominated by what Hegghammer and Lia call "Jihad Strategic Studies." The name is meant to reflect that after September 11, the Islamist discussion is increasingly political rather than religious. This analysis is supported by studies made by the *International Crisis Group* think tank on the basis of extensive field work in Iraq.[180]

The content of online discussions of the case of the Muhammad drawings supports the observation that Jihadists are going through a process of secularization. While high-profile Islamists argued that the blasphemous drawings of the Prophet Muhammad must be met with strong opposition, Jihadists assumed a more pragmatic stance, fearing that the issue might distract attention from the main issues, such as defeating the United States in Iraq and forcing Israel out of Palestine. From that perspective, while the 12 drawings of the Prophet constituted a serious offense against Islam, it was too minor an issue to expend much energy on. At worst, the matter threatened to lead the global Jihad down a wrong cultural path.[181]

Terrorism in Denmark?

The conclusion resulting from the above observations – interesting, possibly surprising, and definitely worrying – is that the conflict and confrontation between the Islamic community of interpretation and the Western liberal-humanist community of interpretation after 9/11 has not been alleviated by the war on terror. On the contrary, it has escalated. Beyond the current zones of conflict – Iraq, Palestine – terrorism is increasingly being organized by local amateurs who derive their identity from virtual communities of interpretation on the Internet. These online communities also serve to compensate for the traditional terrorist training offered in regular camps by providing expert knowledge at the click of a button. Whereas in the 1990s the link between the global and local was provided by talent scouts, today this connection takes place in cyberspace. At the same time it is interesting to note that the ideology, though expressed within an Islamic framework and with reference to Islamic dogma, is becoming increasingly political in terms of strategy as well as content. Yet the most surprising aspect seems to be that, paradoxically, the radicalization of the Islamist community of interpretation is actually leading towards a secularization of Islamism. In other words, the battle over values seems to be more political than religious.

If these conclusions are tenable, as much indicates that they are, then the risk of Denmark falling victim to a terrorist attack is higher today than before and immediately after September 11. Scholars, intelligence agencies and governments in the aftermath of 9/11 concluded that the risk of a terrorist attack on Denmark was small compared to the risk of attacks against the United Kingdom, Spain, the Netherlands, and France. This assessment was based on al-Qaida's modus operandi in the period leading up to 9/11. A consensus was reached that motivation alone was not sufficient for carrying out a terrorist attack; operational capacity was equally important, and compared to London, Rotterdam, Paris, and Madrid, radicalized Islamist communities in Denmark from which Jihadists might recruit were very small. Also, the few such communities in existence here were under heavy surveillance. This premise is no longer valid: the virtual communities on the Internet do not entertain considerations of physical location or membership numbers.

152 — The Globalization of Al-Qaida's Battle over Values

بسم الله الرحمن الرحيم

معسكر البتار

نشرة عسكرية تصدر عن اللجنة العسكرية للمجاهدين في جزيرة العرب – العدد السابع – صفر ١٤٢٥ هـ

في الوقت الذي نرى فيه عباد الصليب يغارون على دينهم وينتقمون لبني جلدتهم ؛ نتعجب أشد العجب من رقاد أمة الإسلام وغفلتها ، فبنوها في كل قطر يسحقون ويقتلون وبلادها في كل يوم تُنتقص والله المستعان .

هذا مع أن دين الإسلام هو دين الوحدة والتعاضد والأمر بنصرة المسلم ظالماً أو مظلوماً ، فما بالكم يا إخوة الدين متخاذلين عن نصرة الإسلام وأهله ؟

أما بكم غيرةٌ على الأعراض ؟ أما بكم حسرةٌ على الماضي التليد الذي صنعه الأجداد البررة ..

إني لأسأل عن قومي ونخوتهم   أين الحمية والأعداء قد جاروا؟
ألا قمبوا لسحق المعتدين لكي   تُشفى الصدور ويُمحى الخزي والعار؟!

- كتائب زهدي
- القافلة تسير ..
- وسيلةٌ ينصر ..
- Uzi
- عذب القبر ..
- العيناء

- الأمن والاستخبارات
- الإعلام والنشاط المضاد
- حرب العصابات
- الأهداف داخل المدن
- المعسكر
- برنامج القوات الخاصة

معسكر البتار - العدد السابع - صفر ١٤٢٥ هـ

Pictured above is a page from issue 7 of the al-Battar, *an online journal founded in Saudi Arabia in 2004 by al-Qaida. The name is a reference to the Prophet's sword, gained as the*

Within these communities is it of no importance whether one lives in Leeds or in the Danish countryside.

The controversy surrounding the publication of the Muhammad drawings in *Jyllands-Posten* are a part of, an expression of, and created by the battle over values taking place on two fronts: an ongoing battle in the Middle East and South Asia between Islamism and Western values, and a similarly ongoing battle between the West and the Islamists. This battle over values has escalated in connection with the war on terror, in which Denmark has shown itself as an active participant, particularly through her participation in the war in Iraq. Obviously going to war entails some risk, of which the Danish government has been aware from the outset, and as a result of which terrorism preparedness levels here were elevated. The question of whether the Muhammad drawings controversy has increased the risk of terrorist attacks on Denmark is impossible to answer. This depends entirely on how the matter is handled in Denmark, and on whether or not a radicalization of the local Muslim immigrant communities takes place. The issue may lead to further confrontation in and polarization of Danish society, or it may lead to more dialogue and better integration. Both these tendencies have emerged in the aftermath of the crisis.

It is very likely, however, that Danish representations abroad will be at greater risk of being targeted in terrorist attacks after the Muhammad

---

spoils of war, which in an earlier age had been used by David to cut off Goliath's head. The sword will see use in the final reckoning at the end of all time. Al-Battar is an alias for Shekih Yusuf al-Ayyiri, a Saudi al-Qaida leader who was killed by Saudi security forces in 2004. The headline reads: "Battar's Camp: Military Decree by the Military Committee for the Holy Warriors in the Arabian Peninsula." It continues: "In this age, when the Crusaders are defending their faith and avenging their brethren in the faith, we are astonished to note the inattention and sleepiness of the Islamic Umma. The sons of the Umma are being destroyed and daily it loses its lands – may Allah protect us. Islam is the religion of cooperation and community, whether the Muslim be the victor or the oppressed. What is wrong with you, oh ye of the faith, who thwart the victory of Islam and the faithful? Have you no sense of honor and property? Do you take no pride in the glorious age of your ancestors?" The issue features articles such as "The Caravan is in Motion", "And the Sword will be Victorious", "The Torture of Speech", "The Security Service and the Intelligence Service – Announcements and Resistance Activities", "The War of the Troops – Inner City Targets", "the Camp – Program of the Special Forces". (Translated from the Arabic by Saliha Marie Fettah. Translated from the Danish by Rune Reimer Christensen and Lea Pedersen.)

cartoon controversy, for the simple reason that Denmark gained a sharper profile as an active party to the global battle over values. An attack on a Danish embassy can now be exploited by Jihadists looking to draw attention to the confrontation between the West and the Islamist cause. In an international perspective, Denmark has lost her innocence. From now on, Danes traveling in the Middle East region will likely be identified with the Muhammad drawings rather than with Danish Lurpak butter. The real reason for this is not a handful of drawings published in a Danish newspaper sometime in September 2005, rather it is that Denmark, along with the rest of the Western world, is party to a morally based war on terror bearing all the hallmarks of a battle over values. In this battle the drawings of the Prophet are merely a welcome excuse for the Islamists to argue their case, which may be summarized as the politicization of Islam and the criminalization of the West. What we are dealing with, then, is a power struggle between Islamism and Western values. War and terrorism are the violent expressions of this battle over values, which is however also expressed in many other ways, including through oral discourse, writing and dialogue. Dialogue is far from always an expression of a common desire to reach an understanding, but often constitutes the expression of a power struggle.

The Kuwaiti televangelist Tariq al-Suwaidah put the point across in *Deadline,* the late-night news report on DR2, on March 10, 2006. He is famous within Islamic communities for encouraging Muslims to contribute to the war against Western civilization. According to al-Suwaidah Western society is doomed to failure, for which reason Muslims need merely supply the straw that will finally break the camel's back. These comments were given at a conference in Canada. On *Deadline* al-Suwaidah declared that Denmark had a choice between apologizing for the drawings of the Prophet or being subjected to a boycott. With great pathos he explained that Muslims in the Middle East had taken to the streets spontaneously due to the Muhammad drawings, because their religious sensibilities had been offended. However, unless the Danish government apologized, he and others like him would use their eminent positions and access to Arab satellite channels to make the Muslim masses take to the streets. In Olso, Mullah Krekar, the exiled leader of the *Ansar al-Islam*, conveyed the same message, as did Anjar Choudary, who succeeded the exiled Omar Bakri Muhammad as head of the London-based *al-Muhajiroun* (renamed the *al-Ghurabaa*): Islam is at war with the West – and vice versa.[182] The very same rhetoric is employed by Danish Muslims such as Ahmed Akkari and Abu Laban, and by the "Muslims in Dialogue" association, which invited the British convert Yvonne Ridley to manage its dialogue with Danish society. None of them can be said to be genuine representatives of Islam or of Muslims, but they exploit the controversy over the drawings of the Prophet with a view to mobilizing adherents of their Islamist ideology for the battle over values being fought within the Middle East and between the Middle East and the West. This is the battle over values in which Denmark got involved through her involvement in the war in Iraq, and whose consequences did not really become apparent to Danes until the drawings of the Prophet Muhammad somehow, in a way that is yet to be determined, ended up in the Arab streets. Now that the Danes as a nation have lost their innocence like a Kierkegaardian Don Giovanni and have been confronted with the ethical choice, the question is how they will align themselves in the global battle over values. Will they seek confrontation, forgiveness or the quiet insistence on the validity of their own values? The Danes call for dialogue, but what are the preconditions for dialogue? This will be the topic of my closing remarks.

Towards a Global Civil War?

Fear the soul and do not cultivate it
For it resembles a vice
Tom Kristensen, in *Havoc*, 1930

On September 11, 1990, George H.W. Bush in an address to Congress announced that, with the rapid waning of the Cold War, a new world order was emerging, under which nations would join forces to combat terrorism and the dissemination of weapons of mass destruction, and to contain ethnic and religious conflicts. Though the speech was made in the context of the budding war against Iraq in 1991, President Bush had grounds for optimism. Superpower rivalry was at an end, the Berlin Wall had been torn down, and the UN system had managed to facilitate a broad consensus regarding the necessity of a military intervention against the Iraqi occupation of Kuwait. As for the Middle East, the peace process was launched with the 1991 Peace Conference and the 1993 Oslo Accords between Israel and the Palestinian Liberation Organization. These developments were ample grounds for an optimism which lasted well into Bill Clinton's first term. The new world order meant the dissemination of democracy through dialogue, cooperation and commitment. It also meant that nations unwilling to cooperate in the establishing of a new world order were met with sanctions (Iraq, Iran, and Afghanistan), or were bombed (Iraq). The bombings of the Iraqi regime in 1996 and 1998 were, however, an indication that the new world order was not right around the corner. In point of fact, as Samuel Huntington argued in an article entitled "The Lonesome Superpower" (*Foreign Affairs* 1999), the world was extremely unstable, suffered from a lack of order and was plagued by innumerable conflicts and regional wars.

Almost 11 years to the day after Bush's speech to Congress another President, bearing the same name, took to the podium announcing a new, comprehensive war which would influence the global situation for many years to come. Nations and peoples of the world were given the choice of joining America in the war on terror or becoming her enemies. "Either you are with us, or you are with the terrorists," Bush announced as he declared war on terror following the events of September 11, 2001. The purpose of the war is to create a new world order in the image of the United States, a global union of free republics based on liberal rights, which embraces democracy as the form of government. A noble objective indeed for those who share these basic values and this vision.

Unfortunately, they are in the minority in the world of today. In the year 2006 only a minority of UN member states deserve to be referred to as democracies. The leadership of the largest member state, China, does not share this vision of a new world order based on human rights and democracy. Certainly not on American terms.

The most active opponent of this vision, the Islamists, interpret it as Western oppression and exploitation, and as an expression of the reign of the infidels. Islamists have suspended all notions of human rights and democracy wherever and whenever they have managed to seize the power to create their own order of society. Such is the case with Iran, for instance, where elections are held but subject to the restrictions imposed by the Iranian Sunni interpretation of Islamic doctrine. It was the case in Afghanistan during the Taliban regime, and remains the case in Saudi Arabia. Liberal rights are conspicuously but quite deliberately absent also in other countries such as Egypt and Syria. These regimes fear their internal Islamic opposition and brutally suppress it, while at the same time occasionally appearing to appease them. In connection with the Muhammad drawings controversy, for instance, Cairo and Damascus allowed the Islamists to take center stage. For this reason alone, one might take pause when well-meaning individuals who usually stand up for human rights chose to listen to Islamist demands for freedom of speech to be curtailed out of respect for the Islamist interpretation of religion – an interpretation which legitimizes the stoning of women, public decapitation, strict separation of the sexes, and zealous mind control. Listening to these people makes no sense. Their ideology must be fought; for the sake of the great majority of Muslims who do not

Towards a Global Civil War?

During a March 2005 visit to Seoul U.S. Secretary of State Condoleezza Rice faced the fact that not everyone welcomes her message of freedom.

embrace the Islamist social order, for the sake of human rights, and for the sake of our Western values.

As we have seen, there are however many indications that the war on terror does not lead to more order, but rather to more Islamism, unrest, terrorism and violence, which in turn lead to calls for civil liberties to be curtailed within Western societies in the name of the all-important war on terror. Extraordinary threats require extraordinary measures, Bush argues, expressing White House approval of the wire-tapping without warrants of American citizens' phones. European governments, including the Danish government, follow suit, in the war abroad as well as in term of counterterrorism legislation at home.

Theory of the Partisan

As the objective of the war is not merely to fight the al-Qaida terrorist agenda which led to the attacks on September 11, but to establish a new global order, this is a far cry from being a regular war between sovereign nations; it rather resembles a global partisan war. It is a war against partisans and terrorists, but also a war fought by means of government-sponsored partisans fighting against rogue states. The best known and most controversial partisan war in recent history took place before the war on terror. The United States supported the Afghan Mujahedin movement in its struggle against the Soviet occupation. But the war on terror has also seen the employment of Afghan partisans, in the form of the so-called Northern Alliance – a huddle of warlords hired by the United States in 2001 to conquer Kabul. There can be little doubt that the United States would support partisans in Iran or even Syria if revolutions were to take place in these countries. This would be consistent with the American cooperation with Kurd militias during the war in Iraq, and the fact that Shia militias were allowed to retain their weapons, which they are now using against Sunni insurgents. The ambiguous legality of classifying Guantanamo detainees as 'illegal combatants' is a direct expression of the nature of the war on terror: it is a partisan war more than it is a regular war between states.

The detainees are not covered by the Geneva Convention statutes for the treatment of prisoners of war, because the circumstances under which they were captured did not qualify them for such treatment; prisoners of war are defined as military personnel in uniform openly carrying weapons, etc., at the time of their capture in open battle. Neither can they be defined as civilians, because they were captured by the Americans during battle. In other words, the detainees at Guantanamo are partisans. Citing international law on the subject of partisans, the United States is trying to build a legitimate legal basis for their indefinite detainment.[183]

In a 1963 article, German political theorist Carl Schmitt argues that partisan wars are much more effective than traditional and regular wars. Examples, Schmitt argues, include the Spanish guerilla movement's war against the French occupation in 1808-13, Napoleon's defeat at the hands of the Russians, and Nazi Germany's defeat at the hands of the Soviet Union.[184] At the same time, he claims that since the Second World War partisan wars seem increasingly to replace regular wars.[185] In his theory of the partisan he characterizes the partisan style of warfare as *irregular*, as opposed to the regular warfare of the modern state-based army which abides by clear and mutually agreed-upon rules of engagement. These rules specify the ways in which war may be waged, how prisoners of war are to be treated, the types of weapons that may be employed, and furthermore that civilian casualties are to be avoided while soldiers must be clearly identifiable as such by their military dress and weapons. The partisan, being irregular in his appearance and methods, undermines the difference between civilians and soldiers. By not adhering to the rules of engagement he becomes unpredictable and difficult to lay down a strategy against. Whereas the partisan is flexible, the regular soldier is bound by rules; consequently the regular soldier labors under restrictions which are too easily transgressed against, for instance when conducting sweeps against the partisan among the civilian population, where the partisan may often successfully hide. In other words, in fighting the partisan the regular army is constantly at risk of committing war crimes. This means that the army is easily criminalized and suffers a loss of legitimacy. This risk of criminalization has increased throughout the 20th century, as international law has come to include a body of legislation on partisan warfare, affording rights to resistance fighters. On the one hand, in the war against the partisan the regular army is forced to employ irregular means that may cost the army its legitimacy, while, on the other hand, the partisan is granted a measure of legality which he may use politically in order to gain legitimacy. This very dissymmetry has been obvious during the war in Iraq, in which the United States has repeatedly been accused of violating the rules of engagement. One example is the intense fighting which took place in Fallujah in October 2005: here, the American forces launched an offensive to fight the insurgents and the terrorists, but as they are visually indistinguishable from civilians, the military offensive took a very heavy toll among civilians, many of whom were either killed, forced to flee the area, or lost their homes to American bombs. As a result of this clear violation of the laws concerning the conduct of war, the United States lost legitimacy, while the insurgents gained an influx of new recruits looking to fight what they see as an illegitimate foreign occupation force. This asymmetry is also the basis for the widespread view in the Middle East and elsewhere that the Israeli army's hunt for Palestinian terrorists is criminal. The more intense the Israeli military efforts against the terrorists, the greater support and legitimacy Hamas comes to enjoy among the Arab populations.

In addition to the concept of irregularity Schmitt attaches three other concepts to the partisan. Firstly, mobility and technological innovation; the partisan always enjoys access to weapons and means of communication because he is able to employ any new innovations in these fields, and because there is invariably a *third party* willing and able to supply weapons and other kinds of support. As discussed earlier in this book, al-Qaida has employed advanced technology, especially IT communication technology, to great effect both before and after 2001. Secondly, unlike common criminals, the partisan always has a *cause*. Thirdly, the partisan is motivated by *the defense of a territory*. The ties between the partisan as an individual and the partisan group are strengthened by the political cause and the necessity of territorial defense: there is a direct correlation between the degree to which the group, or community of interpretation, is under siege, and the degree of legitimacy which his own group enjoys in the eyes of the partisan. This parallels the correlation between the intensity of the Western war on terror and the frequency of terrorist attacks on the West. Mobility, technological innovations, and the presence of Islamists within Western societies mean that the Islamic partisan struggle is not merely a classic defensive war on Islamic soil, but a war of aggression fought in the Western world.

As documented by Schmitt, the war of the partisan is not simply a war waged by irregular means, but also a struggle for legitimacy, that is, a battle over values, a struggle to determine which order will reign within a given territory. The war on terror is by definition global, and it therefore tends towards a global civil war. It is a war against and fought alongside partisans, and it therefore constantly tends to break the rules and relativize the values on which it is based and which it seeks to advance. The worst enemy of the war on terror therefore becomes its own basis of legitimacy: every time the West transgresses against its own rules as part of the war on terror – and the West has no choice but to do so if the war is to be won on the global scale – it loses legitimacy, providing the enemy with the opportunity to enhance its legitimacy. This is exactly the use to which the Islamists have put the Internet, and all reports indicate that they have succeeded. The war on terror has so far led to increasing Islamism and terrorism. One reason for this is that, time and time again, the United States violates or is accused of violating the rules of engagement: Abu Ghraib, Fallujah, Guantanamo, cluster bombs, white phosphorus, secret prisons, and aid and support for irregular militias in Iraq and Afghanistan.[186] Another problem which partisan wars present for democratic states is that they usually develop into lengthy wars of attrition. As the process of de-legitimization takes it toll, the war is decried by the democratic opposition at home. Such is the case with the United States' war in Iraq, which has seen still more members of Congress demand a so-called exit strategy, that is, a plan on how to end the war.

Limits to World Order

The war on terror plays out at the intersection of an idealist vision of a new world order, that is, a community of democratic nations, and the necessities of *realpolitik*, which mean that the West must ally itself with undemocratic nations such as Pakistan and Saudi Arabia, while also creating zones within its own order where the rules do not apply. This is a battle over values as well as a partisan war. If the West continues along this path it will come to a global civil war. This may be won, but the lessons of history indicate that such a victory may be perhaps a hundred years in the making, during which period the West will unavoidably be forced to compromise its own values. The West cannot create a democracy overnight by carrying out a regime change by military means. Such is the lesson of Iraq. Nor can the West create a democracy by forcing through free elections in unfree societies. Such is the lesson of Palestine. In recognition of the fact that the world order preferred by the West is as yet limited to the few rather than the many, rather than forcing through by any means possible a globalization of the Western order the West ought to consider looking inwards as it takes a step back and works to ensure that the values that are supposed to form the basis for the global order are actually preserved as the basis for the Western order; within the Western world as well as in global relations. The idea of a world order is a good one if it serves to regulate the West's own behavior, but bad if it leads to a global civil war. A civil war would force the West to compromise its own values over and over. Our freedom of speech would then be difficult to defend.

Diplomacy follows the turmoil of war; the furthering of democracy through direct economic assistance and support for NGOs who work to improve civil society, the rights of women and the development of a free press. In America, this strategy is called *public diplomacy*; in Denmark, it is called the *Arab Initiative*; the key word is *dialogue.* But no dialogue takes place within a power vacuum. The assumption underlying the dialogue which the West is conducting with Middle Eastern states is that it must lead to democracy and a world order based on democratic states *because* this will increase Western security. That the letter from the 11 ambassadors to the Danish Prime Minister in October 2005 contained language that could be construed as a threat of violence and unrest if Denmark did not agree to engage in a dialogue over the Muhammad drawings might have presented a valid argument for Anders Fogh Rasmussen's refusal to meet with the ambassadors. But this argument is made somewhat ambiguous because the Western dialogue with the Middle East to a very large degree is based on the very concrete threat of military intervention: the *shock and awe* strategy employed against Iraq. This was not only meant to destroy the regime of Saddam Hussein but also to shock the entire region and remind Arab leaders and populations that if they refuse to cooperate with the West in its war on terror they risk a revolutionary regime change orchestrated by the coalition of the willing, meaning the United States and her allies, including Denmark.

It serves as a concrete example that, while a dialogue over the Iranian nuclear energy program is taking place in the UN, a serious discussion on the possibility of conducting a military attack against the Islamic Republic is taking place in Washington and Israel. The prospect of nuclear arms in the hands of an Islamist state such as Iran frightens not only Europe, Israel, and the United States, but certainly also the Arab world and Pakistan. A military attack on Iran, whether carried out as a limited engagement involving the bombing of Iranian nuclear facilities or as a full-fledged regime change effort, will be carried out in the form of a morally motivated pre-emptive strike. A majority of Pakistanis and Arabs would meet it with opposition and resistance rather than cooperation and support. The problem with the morally based war on terror, then, is that it does not lead to more democracy or increased stability, but it does however make it much more difficult to address concrete threats such as the development of an Iranian nuclear bomb.

The moral vision of a world order constituted by democracies, the ultimate objective of the war on terror, is based on the assumption that each and every human being on Earth is possessed of a good, Kantian soul, which salutes Western values and which will manifest itself if allowed to vote in free elections. There is, however, little evidence to suggest that this is actually the case. It must provide food for thought that the countries in which the protests against free speech caused by *Jyllands-Posten*'s Muhammad drawings sounded the loudest and were most violent were the very ones in which Western dialogue, in the holy name of the war on terror, had previously led to reforms and elections: Palestine, Egypt, Saudi Arabia, Pakistan, Yemen, and Southern Iraq. In un-free societies, free elections, controlled elections, and reforms do not seem to lead to support for the project of a new world order, but rather to more enemies of Western values. Instead of proselytizing on behalf of a morally based world order, in the manner of the Spanish *conquistadores* in the Christianization of *el mundo nuevo* – the West might achieve more by lowering the level of its ambitions: it might work to ensure that the rights treasured by everyone, such as the right to personal safety, to an income, and to a measure of influence on the political process, are furthered and improved all over the world. This is a question of economic policy, and the risk is that Saudi Arabia may choose to sell its oil to Asia instead of to the West. But that would be

After the many demonstrations against Denmark had run their course, taking their toll in lost lives, burned flags, and gutted buildings, Danish bishop Karsten Nissen traveled to Cairo to engage in a dialogue with Sheikh Tantawi, head of the prominent al-Azhar Mosque. On his return to Denmark the bishop reported that he felt that they had managed to approach an understanding.

a small price to pay compared to the ramifications of a global civil war in which Islamists and terrorists strive to obtain nuclear weapons and likely end up getting them, because, in this total partisan war, nobody can keep track of who in fact supports whom. The West might miss out on cheap Saudi oil, but it would gain legitimacy and thereby support for the handling and containment of real future threats – this would also equip us better in terms of dealing with future instances of offences against religious sensibilities.

The Islamists call the war on terror a crusade, and it is easy to see why this argument is persuasive in those circles. Danish bishops making a genuine attempt at showing respect for Islam have gone to Cairo brandishing large crosses on their shirts. Meanwhile, Western countries do their utmost to avoid at all cost the showing of any measure of support for Hamas, the winner of what was technically a free election, which only came about as a result of intense Western pressure. Also, the revolution in Iraq is deteriorating into a prolonged and violent conflict. Dialogue or respect for Western values will certainly not result from developments such as these, only more opposition and more enemies. If the West wholeheartedly worked to ensure the creation of a Palestinian state, rather than leaving it up to Israel to define the premises for peace negotiations, and also to ensure that the billions of dollars poured into the Palestinian Authority are carefully managed with a view to ensuring social and economic progress and good governance, rather than ending up in the Palestinian leadership's bank accounts in Europe and the United States, the ensuing balance between idealist vision and practical politics would facilitate the necessary conditions for real dialogue and respect for Western values.

Real dialogue is not about the ecumenical comparison of points of view between Islamists and Danish bishops; it is about cooperation on behalf of the social and political betterment of all. In other words, the West faces a choice between a morally based war on terror, eerily reminiscent of the chaotic Wars of Religion of the late Middle Ages, and a commitment to its own order and its principles in its conduct towards the rest of the world; this might lead to a real and concrete effort at promoting the rights founded in international law. Only this could legitimize the West's defense of its own values, including and perhaps in particular the freedom of speech.

Postscript

After Lebanon: A New Cold War in the Middle East

The war in Lebanon between Israel and Hezbollah in July 2006 foregrounded two tendencies which have characterized the security situation in the Middle East since the 2003 war in Iraq. Firstly, the balance between state and society in the Arab states has become displaced in the sense that the Arab states have been weakened while transnational and oppositional movements based on Islamism have been strengthened. Secondly, after the removal of the regime of Saddam Hussein, Iran's role within the region has been strengthened considerably, and, with their 48 percent share of the seats in the Iraqi parliament and the effective resistance of Hezbollah against the Israeli attack, politically the Shias are now stronger than ever before. The increased strength and significance of Iran and the Shias within the region has brought on the usage among Arab leaders, commentators, as well as Middle East scholars of the term *the Shia Crescent*: a mobilized political zone spanning Iran, Iraq and Lebanon with possible further political potential among Shias in the Arab states in the Gulf and Syria. But this is not expressive of a clear-cut Shia – Sunni confrontation: Sunni imams in the Arabian Peninsula, the Muslim Brotherhood in Egypt, as well as al-Qaida leaders such as Ayman al-Zawahiri have encouraged support for Hezbollah, and the Sunni Hamas in Palestine has joined forces with Hezbollah and is apparently receiving support from Iran. These two tendencies thus seem to merge in a confrontation between, on the one side, a pan-Islamist rebellion against Israel, the West, the U.S. and the American order in the Middle East. This rebellion is led by Iran and Hezbollah and is supported by the otherwise secularized Syria as well as Islamist movements including Hamas, Islamic Jihad, the Muslim Brotherhood, al-Qaida inspired jihadist groups, groups popular within Pakistan, and of course most of the rebels – or terrorists, as it were – in Iraq and Afghanistan. On the other side are Israel, the United States and the Saudi, Jordanian and Egyptian governments which, despite their differing strategic interests and political situations join forces in opposing Iran's strengthened political position within the region, Hezbollah, as well as jihadists and Islamist opposition groups. A picture, then, is emerging of a stronger and more confident Iran, growing popular support for the Islamist opposition movements, as well as weakened Sunni Arab regimes. Countries such as Egypt, Jordan and Saudi Arabia have, since 9/11, come under twofold pressure: from the U.S. and the West in the form of demands that they must fight radicalized Islamism, and by a popularly supported opposition loyal to the Islamist opposition to the U.S. project of creating a new liberal order in the Middle East. The anti-American Islamist opposition has been strengthened by the new media conditions in the Middle East which, with outlets such as *al-Jazeera*, make room for both critical analysis, commentary and reporting of U.S. Middle East policy as well as challenging monopolized media and thereby the flow of information which the Arab regimes have long been able to control through strict censorship of state media outlets. When referring to the Arab regimes as weakened I do not – at least not necessarily – mean to say that their stability has been weakened, but rather that they, in their efforts to control the political discourse within the region, are increasingly challenged by their own oppositions as well as by Iranian agendas.

In addition to this picture, the war in Lebanon led to the Israeli realization that Ariel Sharon's unilateral approach to the Palestinian problem is not viable and certainly no longer enjoys support within Israel. Israelis believe that the failure of the Israeli military to defeat Hezbollah, which throughout remained capable of launching hundreds of missiles onto Israeli territory, was due to the fact that the unilateral Israeli withdrawal from Southern Lebanon in May of 2000 had left Hezbollah, aided by Iran and Syria, free to spend the following six years rearming, building underground military compounds and amassing secret stockpiles of weapons. According to the Sharon plan, which constituted the most important political platform of the Kadima party and led to its March 2006 electoral victory under the new leadership of Ehud Olmert, Israel would unilaterally, meaning without previous negotiations with the

Palestinians, withdraw from the West Bank upon the completion of the so-called security barrier. This plan would allow Israel to define the borders of a new Palestinian state on its own. This would largely coincide with the so-called 'line of June 4' which constituted the border previous to the war of 1967, *except for Jerusalem*, which Israel has subsumed entirely into its own state. The experience of the war in Lebanon has, however, caused support for the plan to plummet, as many Israelis fear a potential rearmament on the Palestinian side of the border similar to that which had taken place in Southern Lebanon. In addition to the widespread criticism directed at the Israeli government over its handling of the conflict and of the subsequent war with Hezbollah, the war has also left the government in desperate need of a plan which might replace the Sharon plan for solving the Palestinian conflict.

Whatever else such an alternate plan might include, it will entail negotiations with Palestinians and Arab states. This necessitates a through revision of Israel's Arab and Palestinian policies. These were designed by Ariel Sharon and have specifically rejected negotiations on the grounds that neither the Arab nor the Palestinian parties were considered fair or, according to Israeli opinion, legitimate negotiating partners – apart from Egypt and Jordan, both of which have entered into peace settlements with Israel and which are both supposed to contribute to any solution of the problem by securing the borders of an eventual Palestinian state. The isolation imposed on Israel in the Middle East, then, results not only from either the policies of the Arab regimes or the popular hostility towards Israel, which for instance is clearly present in Egypt, but also from Israel's own policy, particularly under Ariel Sharon and then carried on by Ehud Olmert until the advent of the war in Lebanon. A policy which up until the war had rejected the Arab Peace Initiative, as promoted by the Saudis and presented to and seconded by the Arab League in 2002, as well as any negotiations with the Palestinian Authority and the governments of Syria and Lebanon. The war both showed and lead to the Israeli realization that Sharon's policy was untenable if lasting and stable security political results were to be reached.

The unilateral Israeli strategy has been supported and facilitated by a U.S. Middle East policy which since 9/11 has likewise prioritized a unilateral approach to the region, based on key concepts such as regime change and the spreading of democracy. As a paradoxical aspect of the American policy, it has turned out that the more vigorously the U.S., on the basis of its new security policy, has engaged itself politically, economically and militarily in the Middle East, the more isolated the U.S. has become within the region. This is true at the societal level where trust in the American superpower is close to zero. It is also true at state level, where the U.S. has renounced the possibility of negotiating with the Palestinian Authority (because it is controlled by a Hamas government), Syria and Iran. The U.S. insists on dictating the conditions for negotiation and cooperation with the so-called moderate Arab states in the form of cooperation regarding the war on terror and, as stated by the U.S. Secretary of State Condoleezza Rice in Jedda in early October, 2006, the fight against extremism, which according to the Secretary means Iran, Syria, Hamas and Hezbollah. This very policy has placed the Sunni Arab states in a difficult dilemma. On the one hand, they are obliged to be loyal to the U.S. with regards to the fight against Islamism, Iran, the Iraqi insurgents, Hamas and Hezbollah. On the other hand, there is growing support among their own populations for exactly this pan-Islamist rebellion, the selfsame forces which the U.S. demands the Arab regimes must cooperate in fighting.

The expectations of the American government that the war in Iraq and the removal of the Hussein dictatorship would initiate a widespread democratization of the Middle East because as free, democratic, liberal Iraq would function as an example to be followed by other states in the region have – unfortunately – far from been fulfilled at this point, four years after the start of the war. On the contrary, the state of security in Iraq is very bad, and 2006 has been the most difficult year since the fall of Saddam Hussein. It is generally acknowledged that Iraq is in fact in a state of civil war, while some, including Kofi Annan, who held the position of Secretary General of the UN until the end of 2006, deem the situation to be worse even than one of civil war. However the Iraqi government and the United States approach the situation, nobody expects Iraq to achieve stability and security, not to mention welfare, prosperity and solid democratic progress, within the foreseeable future. On the contrary, there is widespread concern that Iraq, with or without an American military presence, is bound for an increasingly violent and bloody internal conflict between groups of different political, religious and ethnic affiliations. This outlook is cause for concern not only with regard to the situation in Iraq, but also significantly for the future consequences for the entire region of a deteriorating state of affairs in Iraq. Asher Susser of Tel Aviv University has pointed out that a breakdown of the fragile Iraqi state could have dramatic consequences for the state of Israeli security, as a brutal civil war in Iraq with its attendant refugee crisis could threaten the stability of Jordan, which is already host to more than one million Iraqi refugees. This would extend the conflict to an Israeli frontier state, opening a path to the Israeli border for the enemies of Israel, not least Iran. This perspective constitutes the major contributing factor to Israel's concern over the still deteriorating situation in Iraq. It could strengthen the position and potential of Iran and the Iranian-supported Islamists, including, as previously mentioned, Shia as well as Sunni Muslim groups, as the currently most serious strategic threat to Israeli security. The Iraq crisis, therefore, has ramifications beyond Iraq; it has bearing upon the security of the entire region. The so-called reverse domino theory, according to which democracy would spread from Iraq to the Arabs, as such now threatens to morph into a straightforward domino theory, which sees the spread of violence and insecurity throughout the Middle East. Similar concerns are held by the Saudi Arabian regime which fears that an escalated conflict between Shias and Sunnis in Iraq, with its risk of massacres on Iraqi Sunni Muslims, might mobilize Saudi Sunni Muslim Islamists. This situation could be complicated further if the Saudi Shia minority, possibly supported by Iran, was likewise mobilized by an escalation of the crisis in Iraq.

In addition to the bleak outlook in Iraq, two other civil wars are threatening to break out in the Middle East: in Lebanon the situation remains anything but stable after the last year's war, with Hezbollah refusing to be disarmed as well as demanding greater influence within the Lebanese government; in the Palestinian Authority, the Christmas of 2006 saw earnest violent confrontation between Fatah and Hamas. There is thus a very real risk that three open civil wars could break out in the Middle East in 2007 and, worse still, all three of these may well affect and exacerbate the others. Iran is a factor in all three conflicts. Whatever the nature and significance of the Iranian factor, Israel, the United States and the Arab regimes in Jordan and Saudi arabia insist on interpreting and presenting it as decisive and significant. For this very reason the Baker-Hamilton report recommended that Iran be included in a renewed American diplomatic effort. The premise for this proposal was twofold: firstly, the report establishes that Iran can in fact influence crucial actors in Iraq – referring of course to the Shia Muslim groups behind the Iraqi government – and, secondly, the United States and Iran have a shared interest in preventing the situation in Iraq from deteriorating into a chaotic civil war. The Baker-Hamilton group, officially named *The Iraq Study Group*, is aware that dialogue between the United States and Iran is made impossible by the fact that Iran remains unwilling to comply with American demands that they halt production of enriched uranium. The report therefore suggests that the two issues be separated, leaving the U.S. to negotiate the issue of Iraq with Iran while the nuclear issue is handed off to the five permanent members of the UN Security Council and Germany.

There are, however, several reasons why the suggestions of the Baker-Hamilton report regarding diplomatic negotiation between the U.S. and Iran will not be carried out. Firstly, neither party is ready to separate the two issues, which makes it crucial whether Iran continues its production of enriched uranium. The fact of the matter is that on the issue of Iraq, Iran would be negotiating from a position of strength: the United States is the party which is in trouble, while Iran considers itself to be on the winning side in Iraq. Therefore the Iranians will of course demand something in return for aiding the United States in stabilizing Iraq, and that something will no doubt be that the Americans tone down their demand for the halting of the production of enriched uranium. This is something that neither the Bush administration nor the Democratic congressional majority are willing to surrender. Because neither party is willing to stand down on this issue, it is unlikely that there will be any serious dialogue concerning Iraq. Secondly, there is no basis for assuming that the Iraqi stability desired by Iran resembles the kind of stability desired by the United States. While Iran strategically speaking is pleased with the status quo, the United States wants a more stable and better representative political process, which presupposes much greater inclusion of the Sunni Muslim parties which would certainly weaken the Iranian influence. Stability, then, means one thing in American and quite another in Persian. Thirdly, the Bush administration would have great difficulty – as would a Democratic administration – negotiating the issue of Iraq with the Iranians while Iran overtly not only supports, but in fact gains political leverage within the Middle East by supporting Hezbollah, Islamic Jihad and Hamas. The means of limiting Iran's influence in Iraq and the rest of the Middle East, then, cannot be direct negotiations between the U.S. and Iran – at least not on the basis of the premises on which Iran and a large Washington majority stand firm and which remain mutually exclusive.

The alternative chosen by the Bush administration is to (try to) isolate Iran. This cannot be done by way of the UN due to Chinese and Russian resistance, and, consequently, a revival of the Cold War strategy of containment and deterrence in the form of persistent threats of military action will most likely be the American strategy. The end goal *is not to attack Iran*, but rather to push Iran out of Iraq and the Middle East by forging an alliance between Israel and the Arab countries while, by means of threats of military action, forcing Iran to restrain itself. This Cold War strategy does not exclude diplomatic initiatives such as taking part in multilateral conferences where Iran also participates. It is a well known fact that diplomatic approaches towards the USSR was an integrated part of the Cold Ward strategy as well as initiatives through the UN. But during the Cold War it implied strategic alliances as well as military strength, and so it will vis a vis Iran in the interpretation of the Bush administration. The U.S. military built up in the Gulf during the Winter 2006/2007 and the Secretary of State's efforts to establish an alliance to contain Iran may very well be interpretated in this perspective. Such an alliance would also in the eyes of the Bush administration be useful in creating greater Arab support for the effort to deal with the situation in Iraq. The forging of such an alliance requires the revival of a genuine peace process between the Palestinians and Israel with the clear aim of creating a Palestinian state. If the Arab countries, as intended, are to be included in this process, the basis will be the 2002 Arab Peace Initiative, but even if the U.S. and Israel accede to this, a Palestinian negotiating partner is still absent. Both Israel and the United States prefer Mahmoud Abbas. The problem is that Abbas' position within the Palestinian Authority is weak. He and his party would need to build themselves into not only a genuine but also an attractive alternative to Hamas. The irony of this situation is that the U.S. and Israel together with the Arab countries and the EU now need to rebuild the trust in the Fatah movement and the Palestinian Presidency which the Sharon government since 2001 has systematically dismantled, with a view to implementing his unilateral policy.

Similar problems exist in Lebanon. In terms of security policy the major internal problem here, as in Palestine, is that the government does not have a monopoly on violence, which means that the threat of civil war is a constant presence. Resolution 1701 formed the basis – at least temporarily – for preventing Hezbollah from initiating another war against Israel. But only the disarming of Hezbollah and a strengthening of the government's monopoly on violence can reduce the risk of another civil war. Besides strengthening the government army, the point is to create viable political and social alternatives to Hezbollah for the many Shia Muslims in Lebanon. As long as 30 to 40 percent of the Lebanese population sees the country's social and political situation as guaranteed by Hezbollah, the risk will remain that any attempt at disarming Hezbollah will result in civil war.

A striking analogy exists between Iraq, Lebanon and Palestine: all three stand on the brink of open civil war and the complete breakdown of central government. In all three places the only viable strategy in the effort to stabilize the situation seems to be the creation of strong central state powers possessing a monopoly on violence, and in all three places the massive rebuilding of infrastructure, societal institutions and the creation of impartial and fair systems of justice, welfare and marked improvements in social conditions constitute the only possible way ahead if popular confidence in such central state powers is to be established. None of the three countries can achieve such developments without massive international efforts and as well as the support of the other states in the region. It is therefore sad to note that international and regional support for the establishment of these states and the rebuilding of societies in all three places have been markedly deprioritized if not downright neglected since 2001. In Palestine, the Palestinian Authority has been destroyed since the eruption of the al-Aqsa Intifada in September of 2000 and, not least, the assumption of government in Israel by Ariel Sharon in February of 2001. This development was of course severely exacerbated when the EU and the U.S. cut off funds after the January 2006 assumption of government by Hamas. In Lebanon, political support for the Siniora government which assumed power after the so-called Cedar Revolution in the spring of 2005 has not been followed by international, Western, efforts which, through targeted development projects, for instance in Southern Lebanon, might enable the state to assume responsibility for the social tasks still shouldered by Hezbollah on the basis of Iranian funds. In Iraq, the already weak state totally collapsed in connection with the war: ministries were looted, the army and the police disbanded and local as well as central administration destroyed in connection with the thorough de-Baathification carried out after the dismantling of the regime. Attempts at handling the overwhelming problems of security which followed the fall of Saddam Hussein have largely overshadowed, or hindered, the rebuilding of state and society.

In Palestine as well as Iraq, the West has prioritized the forced implementation of political processes in the form of elections over the rebuilding and establishment of state institutions and society. As in so many other parts of the Middle East, this has led to the strengthening of Islamist forces. In terms of democratization, the Iraq war shows that combining bombs and elections works out poorly; rather than promoting democracy it has strengthened anti-democratic forces and fundamentalism. This is true of places such as Iraq and Palestine, where regime change has been carried out, as well as in countries such as Kuwait and Saudi Arabia, where the governments have carried out tentative political reforms. In other words, free elections in un-free societies within a context of violence and war do not appear to promote either freedom, democracy or political reform. The reason for this probably is that democracy must be viewed as both process and institution. Where the liberal, democratic institutions which constitute the basis for genuinely free elections are absent, elections lead to the releasing of anti-democratic forces rather than to the creation of viable democratic reform processes. Democracy can not likely be established by means of the ballot; experience indicates that it presupposes state institutions which enjoy the trust of the citizens – the voters. These are absent in Iraq, Palestine and, to a great extent throughout the remainder of the Arab countries. In Denmark they were developed and founded during the age of absolute monarchy, and it took another 100 years before the constitutional monarchy of 1848 became a democracy. This does not necessarily mean that the democratization of the Middle East will likewise take a century. The point of departure differs, in the Middle East as well as globally. It does mean, however, that the establishing of relatively well-functioning apparati of state constitutes a necessary premise for the initialization of processes of political reform.

The greatest and most important challenge for the region, and for Western Middle East policy, then, appears to be the creation of apparati of state in Iraq, Lebanon, and Palestine, and the development of the other states in the region. The West needs to engage in politics with the existing Arab states if stability is to be established in the region. Rather than prioritizing political reforms in the form of the carrying out of free elections, the establishment and development of state institutions which command the trust of Middle Eastern and Arab populations must be prioritized by the European Union and the United States if the vision of a new Middle East is to have a chance of being realized. This is not contrary to American and Danish foreign and security policy goals of spreading freedom and democracy to the Middle East; rather, it is an absolute necessity for the achievement of these goals.

Bibliography

Adams, John Quincy (1821): "Warning against the Search for Monsters to Destroy", July 4, 1821

Albright, David & Holly Higgins (2003): "A bomb for the Ummah", *Bulletin of the Atomic Scientists* March/April, Volume 59

Albright, Madeleine K. (2003): "Bridges, Bombs, or Blusters?", *Foreign Affairs* September/October

Al-Rasheed, Madawi (2002): *A History of Saudi Arabia*. Cambridge: Cambridge University Press

al-Zawahiri, Ayman (2001): Knights Under The Prophet's Banner, in Walter Laqueur (ed.): *Voices of Terror. Manifestos, Writings and Manuals of al Qaeda, Hamas, and other terrorists from around the World and throughout the Ages*. New York: Reed Press, pp 426-433

Amin, Samir (1978): *The Arab Nation*. London: Zed Books

Amnesty International (2006): *Beyond Abu Ghraib: detention and torture in Iraq*, March 6, 2006, www.amnesty.dk

Andersen, Christopher (1991): *Madonna*. København. Ekstra Bladets Forlag

Andersen, Lars Erslev (2003): *Den amerikanske orden. USA og det moderne Mellemøsten*, København: Ascheoug

Andersen, Lars Erslev (1991): "at sætte lethed ind mod tyngde – offentlighed, islam og politik i forlængelse af De sataniske vers", *Slagmark* nr. 18

Andersen, Lars Erslev (2004a): "Gidsler, penge, medier og Zarqawi", *Mellemøstinformation* nr. 11

Andersen, Lars Erslev (2004b): "Hjemlandets sikkerhed: Transatlantisk terrorismebekæmpelse før og efter 11. september", in Kenneth Møller Johansen & Terkel Kunding (eds.): *Atlantiske afstande. Samfund, sikkerhed og samarbejde i bevægelse*. København: Akademisk Forlag 2004)

Andersen, Lars Erslev (2005b): "I frihedens navn – krigen mod terror og den retfærdige krigs genkomst, in Carsten Selch Jensen: *Retfærdig krig. Legitimeringer af krig og voldsudøvelse i historien*. Odense: University Press of Southern Denmark (2006)

Andersen, Lars Erslev & Jan Aagaard (2005): *In the Name of God – The Afghan Connection and the U.S. War against Terrorism. The Story of the Afghans veterans as the masterminds behind 9/11*. Odense: University Press of Southern Denmark

Andersen, Lars Erslev (1999): "Khomeinis besværlige testamente", in Lars Erslev Andersen & Jakob Skovgaard-Petersen (ed.): *Satanisk, guddommeligt – og såre menneskeligt. Rushdie-sagen ti år efter Khomeinis dødsdom*. København: Gyldendal

Andersen, Lars Erslev & Marit Flø Jørgensen (2005a): "Landeprofil: Yemen", in Lars Erslev Andersen, Søren Hove, Maj Vingum Jensen (eds.): *Mellemøsthåndbogen. Fakta om landene i Mellemøsten og Nordafrika* Odense: University Press of Southern Denmark

Andersen, Lars Erslev (2005): "Religion, ret og politik i demokratiseringen af Mellemøsten", *Den Jyske Historiker* nr. 110-111
Andersen, Lars Erslev & Peter Seeberg (1999): *Iran. Fra revolution til reform?* København: Gyldendal Undervisning
Andersen, Lars Erslev (2006): "Sårbarhedens retorik – apokalypser i amerikansk terrorismediskurs", in Mia Rendix & Jakob Krohn (eds.): *Amerikanske apokalypser*. Odense: University Press of Southern Denmark
Anonymous (2002): *Through Our Enemies' Eyes. Osama Bin Laden. Radical Islam, and the Future of America*. Washington, D.C.: Brassey's, Inc.
Appignanesi, Lisa & Sara Maitland (1989): *The Rushdie File*. London: ICA
Baer, Robert (2003): *Sleeping with the Devil. How Washington Sold Our Soul for Saudi Crude*. New York: Crown Publishers
Baram, Amazia (2005): *Who are the Insurgents. Sunni Arab Rebels in Iraq*. Special Report 134, United States Institute of Peace, Washington, D.C.
Battle, John, (ed.): *Shaking Hands with Saddam Hussein: The U.S. Tilts toward Iraq, 1980-1984*. National Security Archive Electronic Briefing Book No. 82 (http://www.gwu.edu)
BBC (2001): "Analysis. A Toucher Line?" (On American bombings in Iraq in February 2001) http://news.bbc.co.uk/1/hi/world/middle_east/1174771.stm
Behnke, Andreas (2004): "Terrorising the Political: 9/11 Within the Context of the Globalisation of Violence", in *Millennium. Journal of International Studies*
Bemis, Samuel Flagg (1973): *John Quincy Adams and the Foundations of American Foreign Policy*. New York: W.W. Norton & Co.
Benjamin, Daniel & Steven Simon (2002), *The Age of Sacred Terror*. New York: Random House
Benjamin, Daniel & Steven Simon (2005): *The Next Attack. The Failure of the War on Terror and a Strategy for Getting it Right*, New York: Times Books
Berger, Samuel R. (2000): "A Foreign Policy for the Global Age", *Foreign Affairs* November/December
Bjøl, Erling (2002): *Gyldendals USA-historie*. København: Gyldendal
Blix, Hans (2004): *Disarming Iraq: The Search for Weapons of Mass Destruction*. London: Bloomsbury
Blumenthal, Sidney (2003): *The Clinton Wars. An Insider's Account of the White House Years*. New York
Brandon, James: "In exile, opposition groups unite against Damascus", *The Christian Science Monitor*, November 1 2005
Brisard, Jen-Charles (2005): *Zarqawi. The new face of al-Qaeda*. New York: Other Press
Brown, Dee (2001): *Bury My Heart at Wounded Knee. An Indian History of the American West*. New York: Henry Holt and Co.
Brown, Nathan J. (2004): "Transitional Administrative Law", Commentary and Analysis, March 7/8, 2004. http://home.gwu.edu/~nbrown/
Brozan, Nadine (1994): "Chronicle" (on Claudia Schiffer's dress), *New York Times*, January 25
Burns, John F. & Eric Schmitt (2005): "U.S. generals issue grim outlook on Iraq", *The New York Times*, May 20

Bush, George W. (2003): "President Bush Discusses Freedom in Iraq and the Middle East", Remarks by the president at the 20th Anniversary of the National Endowment for Democracy, United States Chambers of Commerce, Washington D.C., November 6, 2003, http://www.whitehouse.gov/news/releases/2003/11/20031106-2.html

Butler, Richard (2000): *The greatest Threat. Iraq. Weapons of Mass Destruction and the Crisis of Global Security.* New York: PublicAffairs

Chicago Sun-Times (1994): Chanel Fashions with Koran Phrases, January 21

CIA World Factbook (2005), www.cia.gov

Cooper, Jr., John Milton (1983) *The Warrior and the Priest. Woodrow Wilson and Theodore Roosevelt.* Cambridge: The Belknap Press of Harward University Press

Country Reports on Terrorism 2004 (2005): U.S. Department of State, Office of the Coordinator for Counterterrorism, April

The Daily Star (2005): "Iraq draws up plan to privatize state-owned firms. Foreign investors solicited for cash", *The Daily Star*, Lebanon, May 17

Davidsen-Nielsen, Hans & Matias Seidelin (2004): *Danskeren på Guantanamo – den personlige beretning.* København: Politiken

Development Cooperation as an Instrument in the Prevention of Terrorism, Ministry of Foreign Affairs of Denmark, 2003

Diamond, Larry (2004): "What went wrong in Iraq", in *Foreign Affairs* Vol. 83, No. 5 September / October

The Duelfer Report (2004): *Comprehensive Report of the Special Advisor to the DCI on Iraq's WMD*, September 30, CIA, www.cia.gov

Federal Funding to Combat Terrorism, Including Defense Against Weapons of Mass Destruction FY 1998-2001, (http://www.cns.miis.edu/research/cbw/terfund.htm)

Fischer, Michael, M.J. & Mehdi Abedi (1990): *Debating Muslims. Cultural Dialogues in Postmoderny and Tradition.* Madison: University of Wisconsin Press

Gadamer, Hans-Georg (2005): *Truth and Method.* 2nd revised ed. London & New York: Continuum

Gaddis, John Lewis (2004): *Surprise, Security, and the American Experience.* Cambridge: Harward University Press

Galbraith, Peter W.(2003): "Refugees from war in Iraq. What happened in 1991 and what may happen in 2003?", *Migration Policy Institute*: Policy Brief February 2003, No. 2

GAO (2004): *Rebuilding Iraq. Resource, Security, Governance, Essential Services, and Oversight Issues.* United States General Accounting Office Report to Congressional Committees, GAO-04-902R, Washington, D.C.

Gause III, F. Gregory (1999): "Saddam's Unwatched Arsenal", *Foreign Affairs*, May/June

Gerges, Fawaz A. (1999): *America and Political Islam. Clash of Cultures or Clash of Interests?* Cambridge: Cambridge University Press

Graham-Brown, Sarah (1999): *Sanctioning Saddam. The Politics of Intervention in Iraq.* London: I.B. Tauris Publishers

The Guardian, June 7, 2003

Gunaratna, Rohan (2002): *Inside Al Qaeda. Global Network of Terror.* London: Hurst & Company

Halliday, Fred (1996): "The Middle East and International Politics", in Halliday: *Islam and the myth of confrontation. Religion and Politics in the Middle East.* London: I.B. Tauris

Halliday, Fred (2000): *Nation and Religion in the Middle East.* London: Saqi Books

Haugbølle, Sune & Peter Seeberg (2005): "Libanon", in Lars Erslev Andersen, Søren Hove, Maj Vingum Jensen (eds): *Mellemøsthåndbogen. Fakta om landene i Mellemøsten og Nordafrika,* Odense: University Press of Southern Denmark

Hegghammer, Thomas (2005): *Al-Qaida Statements 2003-2004 – A compilation of translated texts by Usama bin Ladin and Ayman al-Zawahiri.* FFI/Rapport-2005/01428, Forsvarets Forskningsinstitutt, Oslo

Hegghammer, Thomas (2002): *Dokumentasjon om Al-Qa'ida – Intervjuer, kommunikéer og andre primærkilder, 1990-2002.* FFI/Rapport-2002/01393, Forsvarets Forskningsinstitutt, Oslo

Henderson, Anne Ellen (2005): *The Coalition Provisional Authority's Experience with Economic Reconstruction in Iraq.* Special report 138, United States Institute of Peace, Washington, D.C.

Henriksen, Anders (2005): "Lovlige og ulovlige kombattanter – fangerne på Guantanamo, Cuba", *EU Ret & Menneskeret* nr. 4, september 2005

Hersh, Seymour M.(2004): *Chain of Command. The Road from 9/11 to Abu Ghraib.* New York: HarperCollins Publishers

Hinnebusch, Raymond (2005): "The Politics of Identity in Middle East International Relations", in Louise Fawcett (ed.), *International Relations of the Middle East.* Oxford: Oxford University Press 2005

Human Right Watch World Report (2006): *U.S. Policy of Abuse Undermines Rights Worldwide,* www.hrw.org

Hume, David, (1998): *Selected Essays.* Oxford: Oxford University Press

Huntington, Samuel P. (1993): "The Clash of Civilizations?", *Foreign Affairs* – Summer 1993

Huntington, Samuel P. (1996): *The Clash of Civilizations and the remaking of World Order.* New York: Touchstone Books

Husted, Poul (2002): "Bushs duer og høge i åben strid om angreb på Irak", *Politiken* September 2, 2002

Høi, Poul (2003): "Spejling: CIA og spejlbilledet i Bagdad", *Berlingske Tidende*, February 13, 2003, 1. sektion, side 8

ICG, International Crisis Group (2005): *Iran in Iraq: How much influence?* Middle East Report No. 38, March 21, www.icg.org

ICG, International Crisis Group (2006): *The Next Iraqi War: Sectarianism and Civil Conflict?* Middle East Report No. 52, February 27, www. icg.org

ICG, International Crisis Group (2006): *In Their Own Words: Reading the Iraqi Insurgency*, Middle East Report No. 50, February 15, 2006, www.icg.org

IDF (2002a): *Large Sums of Money Transferred by Saudi Arabia to the Palestinians are Used for Financing Terror Organizations (particularly Hamas) and Terrorist Activities including Suicide Attacks inside Israel*, TR2-350-02

IDF (2002b): *International Financial Aid to the Palestinian Authority Redirected to Terrorist Elements*, TR2-317-02

Indyk, Martin (2003): "Trusteeship for Palestine?", *Foreign Affairs* May/June
Iraq's Weapons of Mass Destruction – The assessment of the British Government (2002), Downing Street, London, September 24, (www.number-10.gov.uk)
Iraqi Interim Government (2005), Homepage: www.iraqigovernment.org
Jørgensen, Marit Flø & Lars Erslev Andersen (2005a): "Yemen", in Lars Erslev Andersen, Søren Hove, Maj Vingum Jensen (ed.): *Mellemøsthåndbogen. Fakta om landene i Mellemøsten og Nordafrika* Odense: University Press of Southern Denmark
Kant, Immanuel (2004): *Zum ewigen Frieden,* Berlin: Akademie Verlag
Kaplan, Lawrence F. & William Kristol (2003): *The War over Iraq. Saddam's Tyranny and America's Mission.* San Francisco: Encounter Books
Kaplan, Robert D. (1993): *The Arabists. The Romance of an American Elite.* New York: Free Press
Kedourie, Elie (1992): *Democracy and Arab Political Culture.* Washington, D.C.: Washington Institute for Near East Policy
Keegan, John (2004): *Intelligence in War.* New York: Vintage Books
Kepel, Gilles (2002): *Jihad. The Trail of Political Islam.* Cambridge: The Belknap Press of Harward University Press
Kepel, Gilles (2004): *The War for Muslims' Minds. Islam and the West.* Cambridge: The Belknap Press of Harward University Press
Klarskov, Kristian (2006): "Muhammed-tegningerne: Iransk politi hjalp til med angreb på den danske ambassade", *Politiken* 13, February
Knudsen, Tonny Brems (2004): "Slaget om Irak: Konsekvenser for FN og den internationale retsorden", in Kenneth Møller Johansen & Terkel Kunding (ed.): *Atlantiske afstande. Samfund, sikkerhed og samarbejde i bevægelse.* København: Akademisk Forlag 2004
Kornbluh, Peter & Malcolm Burke, eds. (1993): *The Iran-Contra Scandal: The Declassified History.* New York: The New Press
Kupchan, Charles A. & Ray Takeyh (2006): "The wrong way to fix Iran", *Los Angeles Times,* February 26
Laden, Osama bin et al. (1998): Jihad Against Jews and Crusaders. World Islamic Front Statement, 23 February 1998, in Walter Laqueur (ed.): Voices of Terror. Manifestos, Writings and Manuals of al Qaeda, Hamas, and other terrorists from around the World and throughout the Ages. New York: Reed Press, pp. 410-412
Lancaster, John (2004): "India-Pakistan Pact Reflects a New Mode", *Washington Post* January 8
Lewis, Bernard (1988): *The political language of Islam.* Chicago: Chicago University Press
Lia, Brynjar (2006) "Al-Qaeda online: understanding jihadist Internet infrastructure", *Jane's Intelligence Review,* January 1, 2006
Lia, Brynjar & Thomas Hegghammer (2004): "Jihadi Strategic Studies: The Alleged Al-Qaida Policy Study Proceeding the Madrid Bombings, *Studies in Conflict & Terrorism,* 27: 355-375
Litwak, Robert S. (2000): *Rogue States and U.S. Foreign Policy. Containment after the Cold War.* Baltimore: Johns Hopkins University Press
Luciani, Giacomo (2005): "Oil and Political Economy in the international relations of

the Middle East", in Louise Fawcett (ed.), *International Relations of the Middle East*. Oxford: Oxford University Press
Lustik, Ian: "The Absence of Middle Eastern Great Powers: Political "Backwardness in Historical Perspective", i *International Organizations* 51/4
Mehlis Report (2005): Report of the International Independent Investigation Commission established pursuant to Security Council, resolution 1595
Moll, Jakob og Tanja Parker Astrup (2003): "Hvad er meningen: Livshistorie: Storm", *Politiken*, January 1
Mozaffari, Mehdi (1998): *Fatwa Violence and discourtesy*. Århus: Aarhus University Press
Mueller, John & Karl (1999): "Sanctions of Mass Destruction", *Foreign Affairs*, May/June
Mylroie, Laurie (2000): *Study of Revenge Saddam Hussein's Unfinished War against America*. Washington, DC: AEI Press
Myre, Greg (2006): "Olmert lists plans for Israeli borders", *International Herald Tribune*, March 10
Møller, Bjørn (2003): "Irakiske Masseødelæggelsesvåben. Et fiktivt problem" i Clement Behrendt Kjersgaard (red.): *USA/Europa – Fjender i fællesskab?* København: Ræson & Forlaget Halfdan
Napoleoni, Loretta (2003): Modern Jihad. Tracing the Dollars Behind the Terror Networks. London: Pluto Press
National Counterterrorism Center (2005): A Chronology of Significant International Terrorism for 2004. Washington, D.C.
Naveh, Dani (2002): *The Involvemnent of Arafat, PA Senior Officials and Apparatuses in Terrorism against Israel, Corruption and Crime*, Ministry of Parliamentary Affairs, Israel
Nicholson, Emma & Peter Clark (2002): *The Iraqi Marschlands. A Human Environmental Study*. London: Politico's Publishing
Norton, Augustus Richard, ed. (1995-1996), *Civil society in the Middle East*. Leiden: E.J. Brill, vol. I+II
Norton, Augustus Richard (2005): "The Puzzle of Political Reform in the Midle East", in Louise Fawcett (ed.), *International Relations of the Middle East*. Oxford: Oxford University Press
Patterns of Global Terrorism (2000, 2001, 2002, 2003, 2004), State Department, Washington, D.C.
Pedersen, Ove K. (2006): "Danmark år nul", *Information*, February 21
Peterson, Peter G.(2002): "Public Diplomacy and the War on Terrorism", *Foreign Affairs* September / October
Pittelkow, Ralf (2002): *Efter 11. September. Vesten og Islam*. København: Lindhardt og Ringhof
Politiets Efterretningstjeneste (PET 2003): *Årsberetning 2003* (www.pet.dk)
Pollack, Kenneth M (2002).: *The Threathening Storm. The Case for Invading Iraq*. New York: Random House
Pollack, Kenneth M (2004a).: "Spies, Lies, and Weapons: What Went Wrong", *The Atlantic Monthly*, January/February

Pollack, Kenneth M (2004b).: *The Persian Puzzle. The Conflict Between Iran and America*. New York: Random House
"Poul Nielson: USA ude efter Iraks olie", *Politiken,* May 9, 2003
Powell, Colin (2003): *U.S. Secretary of State's address to the United Nations Security Council,* The Guardians hjemmeside (www.guardian.co.uk/Iraq)
Powell, Colin (1995): *A Soldier's Way,* London: Hutchinson
Rappaport, Armin (ed.) (1976): *The Monroe Doctrine*. New York: Robert E. Krieger Publishing Company
Reaching Out to the People of Iran. Fact Sheet, State Department, February 15, 2006
Reeve, Simon (1999): *The New Jackels. Ramzi Yousuf, Osama Bin Laden and the Future of Terrorism*. Boston. Northeastern University Press
Rice, Condoleezza (2000): "Campaign 2000: Promoting National Interest", *Foreign Affairs* January/February
Rice, Condoleeza (2006): "Iran's Nuclear Program", Opening Remarks before the Senate Appropriations Committee Washington, DC, March 9, www.state.gov
Roy, Olivier (2003): "Euroislam: The Jihad within", *The National Interest*, No. 71
Roy, Olivier (2004): *Globalised Islam: The search for a New Ummah,* London: C. Hurst
Rushdie, Salman (1990): *I god tro & Er intet helligt?* København: Samleren
Rushdie, Salman (1988): *De sataniske vers*. København: Samleren
Schlesinger, Arthur J.: *War and the American Presidency*. New York: W.W. Norton 6 Company
Schmitt, Carl (2002): *Det politiskes begreb*. København: Hans Reitzels Forlag
Schmitt, Carl (2004): *Theory of the Partisan: Intermediate Commentary on the Concept of the Political* (1963), Telos nr. 127
Schmitt, Gary J. & Abram N. Shulsky (1999): "Leo Strauss and the World of Intelligence (By Which We Do Not Mean Nous)", in Kenneth L. Deutsch & John A. Murley, eds.: *Leo Strauss, the Straussians, and the American Regime*. Lanham: Rowman & Littlefield Publishers Inc.
Scott, Ronald B. (1993): "Images of Race, and Religion in Madonna's Video *Like a Prayer*: Prayer and Praise", in Cathy Schwichtenberg, ed.: *The Madonna Connection: Representational Politics, Subcultal Indentities, and Cultural Theory*. Boulder: Westview Press
Selch Jensen, Carsten (2006): *Retfærdig krig. Legitimeringer af krig og voldsudøvelse i historien*. Odense: University Press of Southern Denmark
Shoebridge, Charles (2003), "The Gloves Come Off", *The Crime Consultancy* (www.thecrimeconsultancy.com)
Sistani (2005), Ali Sistani's homepage: www.sistani.org
Skovgaard-Petersen, Jakob (1999): "Hvad er de sataniske vers?". Lars Erslev Andersen & Jakob Skovgaard-Petersen (red.): *Satanisk, guddommeligt – og såre menneskeligt. Rushdie-sagen ti år efter Khomeinis dødsdom*. København: Gyldendal
Smith, Tony (1994): *America's Mission. The United States and the Worldwide Struggle for Democracy in the Twentieth Century*. Princeton, New Jersey: Princeton U.P.
Stephanson, Anders (1995): *Manifest Destiny. American Expansion and the Empire of Right*. New York: Hill and Wang

Swisher, Clayton E. (2004): *The Truth About Camp David. The Untold Story About The Collapse Of The Middle East Peace Process*. New York: National Books
Ten Days in Iraq: A Trip Report (2005). Interview with Leslie Gelb & Richard Haass. Transcript. Council of Foreign Relations, April 26, www.cpr.org
Tenet, George (2003): *The Worldwide Threat in 2003: Evolving Dangers in a Complex World*. Testimony of Director of Central Intelligence George Tenet, before the Senate Select Intelligence Committee, February 11
Tripp, Charles (2002): *A History of Iraq*. Cambridge: Cambridge University Press
TV2 Nyhederne website (2006): Bush truer Iran, March 12, 2006
Tønnesen, Truls H. (2006): *Jihadist Reactions to the Muhammad Cartoons*. Working Paper, presentation FFI, Oslo, March 15, 2006
Ullman, Harlan K. & James P. Wade (1996): *Shock and Awe, Achieving Rapid Dominance*. Washington, DC: National Defense University Press
UNDP (2005): *Arab Human Development Report 2004. Towards Freedom in the Arab World*
UNDP (2005): *Iraq Living Conditions Survey 2004*. Vol. 1: *Tabulation Report*; Vol. 2: *Analytical Report*; Vol. 3: *Socio-Economic Atlas*, UNDP, New York (www.undp.org)
USIP (2004): *Iraq's Constitutional Process. Shaping a Vision for the Country's Future*. Special Report 132, United States Institute of Peace, Washington, D.C.
"USA indrømmer oliekrig", *Politiken*, June 5, 2003
"USA's viceforsvarsminister misforstået", *Politiken*, June 11, 2003
The Washington Post (2005): "Quality of Life Deemed Poor in Iraq", *Washington Post*, May 17
Whitaker, Michael & Brian (2003): "UK war dossier a sham, say experts. British 'intelligence' lifted from academic articles", *The Guardian*, February 17
The White House (2002): *The National Security Strategy of the United States*, 2002
The White House (2005): *National Strategy for Victory in Iraq*, November 30, 2005
Wiktorowitz, Quintan (2001): "The New Global Threat: Transnational Salafis and Jihad", *Middle East Policy*, no. 4, December 2001
Wittes, Tamara Cofman, ed. (2005): *How Israelis and Palestinians Negotiate. A Cross-Cultural Analysis of the Oslo Peace Process*. Washington, D.C.: United States Institute of Peace Press
Woodward, Bob (2004): *Plan of Attack*. New York: Simon & Schuster
Woodward, Bob (2002): *Bush at War*. New York: Simon & Schuster
Woodward, Bob (1991): *The Commanders*. New York: Simon & Schuster
World Bank (2004): *Reconstructing Iraq. Documents of The World Bank*. Working Paper Series. Executive Summaries, October 1
www.intelcenter.com/
www.siteinstitute.org/
Zayno, Sheikh Muhammad Bin Jamail: *Bogen om den sejerrige gruppe & dens metodelære*. Oversat af Murad Storm Ad-Danemarki, Sanaa: Universities Publishing House
Zilmer-Johns, Lisbet (2004): *EU og terror*. Rapport fra Institut for Internationale Studier. København: DIIS

Notes

1. Pedersen (2006)
2. Huntington (1993); Huntington (1996)
3. See Andersen & Aagaard, *In the Name of God* (2005) for a further discussion of the term 'fundamentalism'
4. On the basis of Hans-Georg Gadamer's philosophical hermeneutics as outlined in his *Truth and Method* (1960, see Gadamer 2005), philosophers such as Richard Rorty and Stanley Fish developed the concept 'communities of interpretation'
5. Al-Madawi (2004)
6. Hiro (2002)
7. On Salafism, see Wiktorowitz (2001)
8. See Kepel (2002) on Nasser and the Muslim Brotherhood
9. Kepel (2004)
10. Andersen, Christopher (1991)
11. Ibid.
12. An English translation of the verse would be: "They are the ones who found guidance", which appears repeatedly in the Koran
13. See Skovgaard-Petersen (1999) for an outline of the controversy and a discussion of the significance of *the Satanic Verses*
14. Andersen (1991)
15. I rely on Fischer & Abedi's very interesting account of the living conditions of British Muslims around the time of the publication of *the Satanic Verses*: Fischer & Abedi, *Debating Muslims. Cultural Dialogues in Postmodernity and Tradition* (1990). For extensive analyses of the Rushdie affair, see my articles: Andersen (1991) and Andersen (1999)
16. Fischer & Abedi p. 385
17. A collection of sources on the Rushdie affair, including Rushdie's statement of regret, have been published in Appignanesi & Maitland (1989). Rushdie outlined his views on the freedom of expression, religion, and art in two essays published in 1990, "In Good Faith" and "Is Nothing Sacred?"
18. On Danish-Iranian relations 1989-1992, see Andersen & Seeberg (1999) and Mozafarri (1998)
19. Mozaffari (1998)
20. Part 1 is based partly on my article, "USA og Mellemøsten under George Bush", in Andersen, Hove & Vingum (eds.), *Mellemøsthåndbogen* (2005)
21. President Bush Discusses Iraq Policy at Whitehall Palace in London, Remarks by the President at Whitehall Palace Royal Banqueting House-Whitehall Palace, London, England, November 19, 2003
22. See e.g. Gergers (1999), and Litvak (2000)
23. Rice (2000); Powell (2001)
24. The White House (2002)
25. Andersen (2003)

26. Ullman & Wade (1996)
27. Wittes (2005)
28. Peterson (2002)
29. Schlesinger (2004)
30. Albright (2003a)
31. Selch (2006)
32. Andersen (2001)
33. BBC (2001)
34. It is a well known fact that Clinton in 1996 and 1998 ordered military campaigns in Iraq, but after Operation Desert Fox in 1998 no military actions was ordered by the Clinton administration
35. Blumenthal (2003), 780
36. For an in-depth analysis see the chapter "Den strategiske allierede – USA og den israelsk-palæstinænsiske konflikt" in my book *Den amerikanske Orden. USA og det moderne Mellemøsten* (Copenhagen: Aschehoug, 2003)
37. Oddly enough, this frantic hoarding did not occur at all in 2004 and 2005, when oil prices soared even higher
38. This was established in the State Department's annual report on *Patterns of Global Terrorism*
39. e.g. Mylroie (2000)
40. For a clear presentation of the debacle over the ineffectuality of the sanctions, see F. Gregory Gause III, "Saddam's Unwatched Arsenal", and John & Karl Mueller, "Sanctions of Mass Desctruction", in the May/June 1999 issue of *Foreign Affairs*. After the war, a UN inquiry indicated that the UN system itself was largely to blame for the problems which plagued the Oil for Food Program
41. Though the United States played a leading part in enforcing the sanctions, it received the heartfelt support of a number of countries including Denmark, which unlike France fully endorsed the U.S. policy towards Iraq for the entire duration of the Program
42. The British scholar on Iraq, Charles Tripp, argues convincingly that sanctions are based on the notion that a will to democracy always exists amongst any population; if sufficient pressure is exerted against its government, the people will rise and demand democracy
43. After assuming the office of Secretary of State, Colin Powell sought to continue President Clinton's diplomatic UN policy, to no avail. The attempt to impose 'smart sanctions' did not find any support with China, France, and Russia, three permanent members of the Security Council
44. Pollack (2002)
45. Bulter (2000)
46. In a Danish context, this argument has been advanced by Bjørn Møller, for instance in his article "Irakiske Masseødelæggelsesvåben. Et fiktivt problem?", in Clement Behrendt Kjersgaard (ed.), *USA / Europa – Fjender i Fællesskab?* (Copenhagen: Ræson & Forlaget Halfdan, 2003). Cf. this book for a number of interesting articles and interviews on trans-Atlantic relations in the light of the Iraq conflict

47. See e.g. Poul Husted: "Bushs duer og høge i åben strid om angreb på Irak", *Politiken*, September 2, 2002. General Anthony Zinni, Commander in Chief of U.S. Central Command from 1997-2000 stated his views at the Center for Defense Information in Washington, D.C. on October 31, 2002 (http://www.cdi.org)
48. See e.g. Joyce Battle (ed.): *Shaking Hands with Saddam Hussein: The U.S. Tilts toward Iraq, 1980-1984*. National Security Archive Electronic Briefing Book No. 82 (http://www.gwu.edu)
49. Woodward (1991): Kaplan (1995)
50. Schmitt & Shulsky (1999)
51. Ibid. The concept of "mirror imaging" is, with reference to Eliot Cohen, introduced in this article: it describes the act of projecting one's own mindset onto the enemy. In a 2003 article in *Berlingske Tidende*, journalist Poul Høi ridiculed me for being afflicted with "mirror imaging" for expressing to the Ritzau News Agency some doubt as to the validity of the evidence presented by Colin Powell at the UN Security Council meeting in February 2003. On that occasion Powell "documented" the existence of Iraqi programs for the development of weapons of mass destruction, as well as Iraq's collaboration with al-Qaida. These three years later one may speculate as to who did and who did not suffer from "mirror imaging". One could chose to refrain from such speculation and merely observe that one must employ such philosophical terms derived from textual theory with great care when assessing one's enemies. Høi (2003)
52. On September 24, 2002, the report *Iraq's Weapons of Mass Destruction – The assessment of the British Government* was made available by the Prime Minister's Office. It is available for download at www.number-10.gov.uk
53. See e.g. Michael & Brian Whitaker: "UK war dossier a sham, say experts. British 'intelligence' lifted from academic articles", *The Guardian*, February 7, 2003
54. Blix has subsequently expressed a critical view of the quality of the information on Iraq made available by Western intelligence agencies. Cf. Blix 2004
55. *U.S. Secretary of State's Address to the United Nations Security Council*, February 5, 2003, is widely available on the Internet. See, for instance, *The Guardian*'s website (www.guardian.co.uk/iraq)
56. Knudsen (2004)
57. Cf. "Poul Nielson: USA er ude efter Iraks olie", *Politiken*, May 9, 2003: "I think this is an attempt by the United States to join OPEC. They are monopolizing the oil."
58. Kaplan & Kristol (2003)
59. Woodward (2002)
60. The Duelfer Report (2004)
61. Country Reports on Terrorism 2004 (2005)
62. For an in-depth analysis see the chapter on Iraq
63. Ten Days in Iraq (2005)
64. *Office of Special Plans*, see Seymour M. Hersh (2004) and Pollack (2004)
65. Burns & Schmitt (2005)
66. Kaplan & Kristol (2003, 98f)
67. The Pentagon flatly rejected the State Department's blueprints for a post-war Iraq. These plans, developed by the Future of Iraq Project, were made on the basis of

detailed analyses of a post-war situation; according to sources in Washington, these analyses have turned out to predict post-war problems quite accurately
68. Woodward (2004)
69. Pollack (2004b, 354f)
70. Henderson (2005)
71. Galbraith (2003)
72. Graham-Brown (1999); Pollack (2002a)
73. Henderson (2004)
74. Ibid.
75. Ibid.
76. Ibid.
77. ICG no. 52 (Draft 2006). For my account of developments in Iraq I am indebted to the unique scholarship of the International Crisis Group (ICG)
78. Tripp (2002, 264ff)
79. Kepel (2004)
80. Ibid.
81. Ibid.
82. Ibid.
83. Kepel (2004). See the thorough USIP report on Iraqi insurgents by Amazia Baram, an Israeli expert on the Iraqi insurgency. Baram (2005)
84. Kepel (2004)
85. Ibid.; Tripp (2002)
86. ICG br. 52 (2006)
87. Ibid.
88. Sunni Arabs achieved representation on the constitutional preparatory committee, despite having boycotted the January parliamentary elections. However, Sunnis were not party to the draft constitution as they proved unwilling to accept the compromise between the Kurd and Shia factions. Nevertheless the decision was made to put it to a referendum as the number of Kurd and Shia Muslim voters was sufficient to potentially pass the compromise
89. ICG no. 52 (Draft 2006)
90. Brisard (2005)
91. ICG no. 50 (2006); Lia & Hegghammer (2006)
92. The White House (November 2005)
93. There are several competing theories of why the Camp David negotiations collapsed. See e.g. Wittes (2005); Ross (2004); Swisher (2004)
94. IDF Reports (2002a & 2002b); Naveh (2002)
95. The United States, the EU, the UN, and Russia
96. Indyk (2003)
97. During the March 2006 general election Ehud Olmert, who recently succeeded Ariel Sharon as Prime Minister of Israel, repeatedly confirmed that the Kadima Party would carry out the Sharon plan, thereby imposing by force the unilateral Israeli definition of the border between Israel and a future Palestinian state. Cf. *The International Herald Tribune*, "Olmert lists plans for Israeli borders", Myre (2006)

98. Syria Accountability and Lebanese Sovereignity Restoration Act, http://www.21a.org/lebanon/syriac2003.htm
99. Haugbølle (2005)
100. Mehlis (2005)
101. Brandon (2005)
102. Kornbluch & Byrne (1993)
103. Pollack (2004)
104. Steven R. Weisman: "U.S. and Europe Are at Odds, Again, This Time Over Iran", *New York Times*, December 12, 2004; "Facing Iran", *Washington Post*, December 6, 2004
105. Given the Iranian reaction to the Muhammad drawings – demonstrators calling for 'Death to Denmark', the burning of Danish flags, and the use of incendiary bombs against the Danish Embassy – describing the Iranian response as relatively moderate may seem inappropriate. The true scale of measurement, however, must be the number of actual death threats and the possibility that demonstrators might occupy the Embassy. On the relationship between the police and the demonstrators, see the eye witness statement quoted in *Politiken* (Klarskov 2006)
106. Rice (2006)
107. TV2 Nyhederne [Danish television news program] (2006)
108. Kupchan & Takeyh (2006); Rice (2006)
109. The most straightforward solution would be negotiations between the United States and Iran. Such indeed took place prior to the war in Iraq. However, solving the problem of Iran's nuclear energy program requires that agreements are forged for a new security situation in the Gulf. This is unlikely to happen in the near future
110. Part 2 is partly based on Andersen (2005)
111. Kant (1995)
112. See Rappaport (1976) on the Monroe Doctrine
113. Stephanson (1995)
114. Bemis (1973)
115. Bjøl (2002); Cooper (1983); Gaddis (2004); Smith (2004)
116. In a Danish context it seems highly provocative to call the American confrontation with Native Americans a process of ethnic cleansing and genocide. Nevertheless one would be hard pressed to find any American historian in the Academy, even a conservative one, who would deny that the history of U.S.-Native American relations is a particularly grim chapter of American history
117. Cooper (1983)
118. Andersen (2003)
119. UNDP (2005)
120. Andersen (2003)
121. Kedourie (1992); Lewis (1988); Pittelkow (2002); Norton (2005)
122. Andernen & Aagaard (2005)
123. Norton (2005); Kepel (2004)
124. This theory was developed in the early 1970s by scholars such as the Egyptian social scientist Samir Amin, on the basis of Marxism and the critique of imperialism. Amin (1978)

125. Luciani (2005). Taking a critical view of his own theory, Luciani recognizes that the smaller Gulf States have experienced a high degree of economic privatization which allows a greater degree of influence over political decision making processes. However, though countries such as Kuwait and Qatar have carried out such processes of reform these have not amounted to an actual process of democratization
126. Hinnebusch; see also Halliday (2000)
127. Powell (1995)
128. Gerges (1999)
129. Halliday (1996)
130. Jørgensen (2005)
131. Zindani also made headlines when he demanded that a Yemenite newspaper editor then under indictment for publishing the Muhammad drawings be executed
132. Interestingly, Danish translations of Yemenite Salafi Islamist tracts have been made available by Murad Storm, a Danish convert and former member of the Bandidos Motorcycle Club. Storm studied Islam under Zindani, who also taught the "American Taliban" John Walker Lindh. On Murad Storm cf. Jakob Moll & Tanja Parker Astrup (2003). On Storm's translations, see Zayno
133. For an in-depth analysis, see Andersen (2005a)
134. Gerges (1991)
135. Ibid.
136. See Andersen (2005b) for an analysis of the war on terror as the return of just war
137. Baer (2003)
138. Of the 19 hijackers 15 were Saudis, two were Emiratis, one was Lebanese, and one was Egyptian
139. Part 3 is based on my article "Mellemøsten og al-Qaida", in Andersen, Hove & Vingum (eds.), Mellemøsthåndbogen (2005)
140. Andersen (2004)
141. Since the late 1990s, the United States government has proposed theories on a new type of terrorism, known variously as postmodern terrorism, super-terrorism, WMD terrorism, etc. This discussion, however, was largely confined to a limited number of experts, the federal government, and D.C. lawmakers
142. De-politization is a term developed by German political theorist Carl Schmitt (2002). Behnke (2004) provides an outstanding and inspiring analysis of the discussion of the new terrorism, informed by the concepts of de-politization and Schmitt's theory of the partisan
143. Country Report (2005)
144. Andersen (2004)
145. Berger (2000)
146. Andersen (2004)
147. It is worth noting that political disagreement over Iraq has proved no hindrance to European or American initiatives to further develop the paradigm of homeland security which was founded by the Clinton Administration and stepped

Bibliography and Notes 193

148. This new focus on the terror threat and the countermeasures it has prompted is quite a costly one. According to a May 2005 analysis by the Homeland Security Research Corporation, a D.C.-based think tank, in 2005 world governments spent a combined $191 billion on counterterrorism measures. U.S. spending accounts for 44 per cent of this total. Spending is expected to rise to $517 billion by 2015. For purposes of comparison, if the Millennium Development Goals (which are to fight poverty worldwide etc.) are to be reached by 2015, the UNDP calls for an annual $135 billion in 2006, rising to $195 billion by 2015. (More information at www.undp.dk). To put this in perspective, in April 2005 the newly-formed United States National Counterterrorism Center put the number of casualties from terrorist attacks worldwide throughout 2004 at 1907, on the basis of the enhanced U.S. information-gathering capabilities (cf. National Counterterrorism Center, 2005qq). Following changes in its information-gathering methodology, the Center in June 2005 updated the number to 28,433 dead, wounded, or kidnapped
149. Cf. Zilmer-Johns (2004) for an overview of EU initiatives
150. Kepel (2004); Anonymous (2002)
151. At the time of publication Scheur was still with the CIA, and it was therefore published anonymously. Following the publication of his second book, *American Hubris*, Scheur left the CIA and allowed his name to become publicly known
152. Anonymous (2002)
153. See Andersen & Aagaard (2005) for a detailed account
154. Gunaratna (2002)
155. Keeping in mind the U.S. failure in Vietnam, the withdrawal of U.S. forces from Lebanon in 1983 following an attack on U.S. Marines by the Hizbollah, and the fact that Afghan forces successfully managed to eject Soviet forces from Afghanistan, this project was considered feasible
156. al-Zawahiri (2001: 430): "The one slogan that has been well understood by the nation and to which it has been responding for the past fifty years is the call for the jihad against Israel. In addition to this slogan, the nation in this decade is geared against the U.S. presence. It has responded favourably to the call for the jihad against the Americans."
157. Kepel (2004)
158. It must however be emphasized that examples do in fact exist of Islamists who have unequivocally argued for the Islamization of the entire world, such as for instance Omar Muhammad Bakri, the founder of the London based al-Muhajiroun Party, as well as his successor, Anjem Choudary
159. Hegghammer (2002); Hegghammer (2005)
160. Osama bin Laden quoted in Hegghammer (2002)
161. Anonymous (202)
162. al-Zawahiri (2001)
163. Kepel (2004)
164. al-Zawahiri (2001)

165. Andersen (2004a)
166. Terrorist Financing (2002)
167. See Napoleoni (2003) for a quite different assessment
168. In his book *Danskeren på Guantanamo* Slimane Hajd Abderrahmane, a Danish citizen detained at Guantanamo for 747 days, describes the process by which a person seeking to participate in e.g. the Chechnyan struggle may be recruited Cf. Davidsen-Nielsen & Seidelin (2004)
169. PET (2003)
170. Reeve (1999)
171. Roy (2004); Kepel (2004)
172. The main difficulty encountered by states seeking to combat irregular partisans and terrorist networks such as al-Qaida is that the opponent is unpredictable and employs all manner of illegitimate means. This is part of the basis for the asymmetry. Recently, the Abu Ghraib scandal brought attention to the problem that a state might begin to imitate the terrorist network it seeks to destroy. This process of imitation can lead to a de-legitimization of the state and, paradoxically, a legitimization of the network, as the latter can claim that the state is breaking the rules it ostensibly fought to uphold
173. Lancaster (2004)
174. David Albright (2003)
175. Tenet (2003)
176. Benjamin & Simon (2005)
177. Roy (2003). For a more in-depth analysis see Roy (2004)
178. Lia (2006)
179. See Andersen (1991) for an analysis of the Rushdie affair in relation to European written culture
180. Lia & Hegghammer (2006). Their analyses are largely borne out by International Crisis Group analyses of Islamist communication and discussions in Iraq. ICQ no. 50
181. Tønnesen (2006)
182. Cf. an interview with Mullah Krekar published in *Dagbladet* (Oslo) and on the al-Ghurabaa website. Tariq al-Suwaida's analysis of the clash of civilizations can be found on the Young Muslims' website
183. Cf. Henriksen (2005)
184. Carl Schmitt was a Nazi, a party member throughout, and a functionary of the Nazi state. He remains controversial, and parts of his work are clearly influenced by his background. At the same time his work continues to bear the hallmarks of a highly original, widely read and incisive mind. In recent years Schmitt has been rediscovered and has become a source of inspiration to many who could and cannot possibly be accused of harboring Nazi sympathies. On his theory of the partisan, see Schmitt (2004). See also Behnke (2004) for a thought-provoking analysis of the war on terror inspired by Schmitt's theory
185. With respect to the United Kingdom, this observation is supported by the renowned British military historian John Keegan. (Keegan 2002: 399ff)
186. Amnesty International (2006); Human Rights Watch (2006)